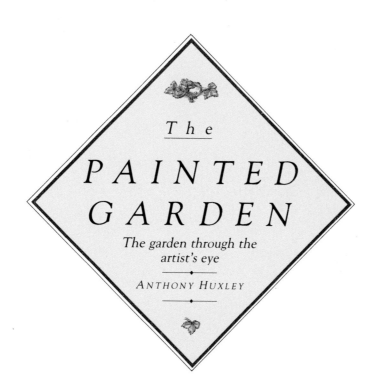

The

PAINTED GARDEN

The garden through the
artist's eye

ANTHONY HUXLEY

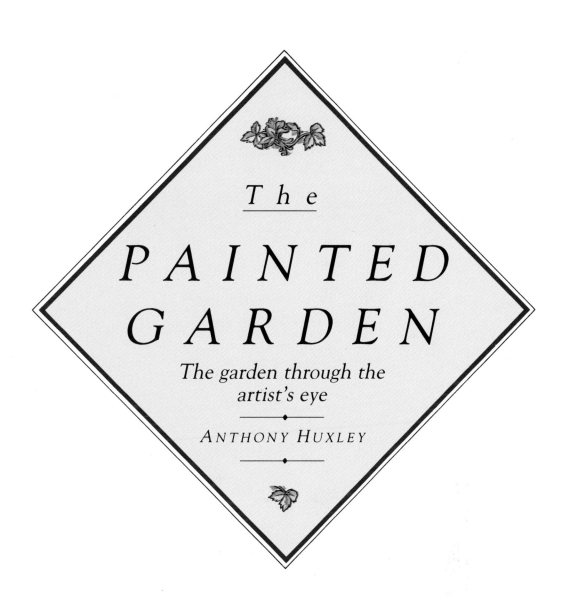

The

PAINTED
GARDEN

The garden through the
artist's eye

ANTHONY HUXLEY

WINDWARD

For my wife, Alyson

A QUARTO BOOK

WINDWARD
an imprint owned by W H Smith and Son Limited
Registered No 237811, England
Trading as W H Smith Distributors
St John's House, East Street, Leicester LE1 6NE

ISBN 0 7112 0540 3

This book was designed and produced by
Quarto Publishing plc
The Old Brewery
6 Blundell Street
London N7 9BH

PROJECT EDITOR: Susan Berry
EDITOR: Hazel Harrison

DESIGNER: Peter Bridgewater
DESIGN STYLIST: Ursula Dawson

ILLUSTRATOR: Vana Haggerty

PICTURE RESEARCHER: Celestine Dars

ART DIRECTOR: Moira Clinch
EDITORIAL DIRECTOR: Carolyn King

Typeset by CST, Eastbourne
Manufactured in Hong Kong by
Regent Publishing Services Ltd
Printed by Leefung-Asco Printers Ltd, Hong Kong

Frontispiece: The Cactus Fancier *by Carl Spitzweg*

CONTENTS

INTRODUCTION

Entitled 'Three Princesses in a Garden' this 15th-century impression of a Persian garden includes flowering trees, a stream running sinuously around them, and flower-spangled turf – the 'flowery mead' of the medieval gardens of Europe. (Bibliothèque Nationale, Paris)

The foremost pleasure in garden paintings lies, perhaps, in their intrinsic beauty, but for the gardener the interest and beauty of the scenes they show, and the record they form of the development of garden design, follow close behind.

The paintings presented in this book are, in the main, records of gardens as they actually were. Sometimes – as in those depicted in the *Romaunt de la Rose* – they may be gardens of the poetic imagination, but even these, allowing for various degrees of stylization, still represent the characteristic gardening design of the times.

Several centuries elapsed before painting became more imaginative than realistic, in the hands of the Impressionists and various more recent artists.

Gardening and art have, in fact, been linked for several thousand years, notably in the countries where gardening really began: Egypt and China. In the latter, above all, 'landscape painting and gardening are so intertwined in their development that it is hard to appreciate the one without knowing something of the other. Both arts developed together, painters providing several of the conventions through which the Chinese looked at their gardens, and gardens in turn giving back these conventions to painters.' (Maggie Keswick, *The Chinese Garden*)

The fashion for landscape painting undoubtedly influenced the vogue for the landscape garden in the late 17th century. Another example of painterly influence is that of the Frenchman, Hubert Robert, who both depicted and designed rococo gardens in the late 18th century. Later still William Morris with John Ruskin helped direct gardening trends, while the painter Gertrude Jekyll actually became an influential garden designer.

As Mac Griswold points out in *Pleasures of the Garden*, 'gardens do closely resemble paintings, with foreground, middle and background, as well as planned perspectives. Garden designers, like painters, often use framing devices . . .' in compositions which 'depend for their effect on light, shade and distance.'

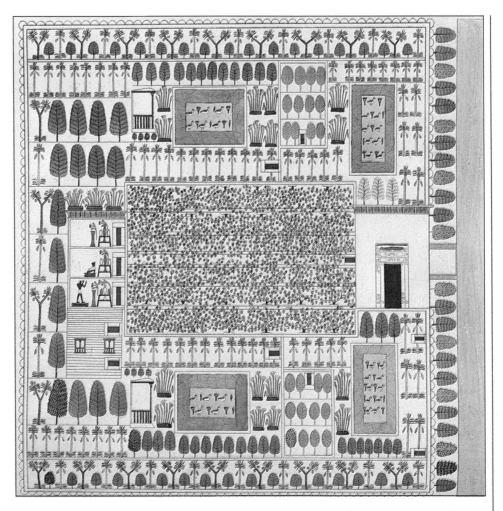

The garden here is that of a high Egyptian official of the Pharaoh Amenhotep III, in about 1400 BC. Though mainly utilitarian, this typically elaborate formal layout includes sitting pavilions by two of the papyrus-fringed pools, and many fruiting trees, including date and doum palms, and a row of shade-providing trees by the entrance to the right. The centre is filled with trained vines. (British Library, London)

THE DEVELOPMENT OF GARDENING

Painting and sculpture are, of course, much earlier art forms than gardening, even if their earliest manifestations in Palaeolithic art were primarily for ritual purposes. Gardening could not, after all, begin until the hunter-gatherers and, later, the nomadic herders settled in one place, built homesteads and made enclosures.

Most early gardening was devoted to growing plants useful as medicinal herbs, vegetables and fruit, and the early accounts of gardening are often concerned primarily with the plants grown, especially the herbs. Man's association with, and dependence on, plants has resulted in their being depicted on countless occasions in engravings, reliefs, frescoes and other paintings; but only gradually did representations of actual gardens emerge, as the garden transcended its utilitarian role to become an art form in its own right.

Little by little gardens became formalized for the pleasure of the occupants of the house, and plants were grown and

All the classic ingredients of the Indian garden are here – lush planting of exotic trees and colourful flowers, an elaborate fence around a terrace and, above all, a rectangular pool with a fountain providing the sound and movement of water, as well as much needed coolness in a hot climate. (Victoria and Albert Museum, London)

appreciated for their decorative qualities, mainly in the homes and estates of the rich and powerful who have left us written or drawn and painted evidence of the earliest gardens.

In ancient Egypt, Mesopotamia, and China, from around the second millennium BC, there are written records of gardens. Egypt has left us tomb paintings from the same period, which, although religious in their application, were artistic representations of gardens as they must have been then.

The first paintings of Chinese gardens date from about the 8th century AD, although their history, as already suggested, is much older, having evolved there from game parks which their owners enclosed and planted with exotic trees. Japan followed the Chinese example, and developed and refined it – in a more austere and impersonal way – from about the 6th century AD.

In India decorative gardening, again very much the province of potentates, began around the 4th century BC. Centuries later, Islam, the religion founded by Mohammed in the 7th century AD, was one of the most influential civilizations in gardening terms. In Persia, gardens had started with parks or enclosures known as *pairidaeza* – game and tree parks like those of the Chinese. Under Islam they developed very characteristically into formal layouts (oases in the heat of the plains) with avenues or water channels typically arranged in a cross pattern – a widespread religious symbol that recalls the words of Genesis, 'a river went out of Eden to water the garden; and from thence it parted, and became four heads'.

The Islamic gardening tradition, with gardens full of trees, shrubs and flowering plants, spread to North Africa in the 9th century, to Spain in the 10th, and Turkey in the 15th, and in the opposite direction to Central Asia from whence, under Mughul rulers, it spread to Afghanistan and the parts of India which were conquered.

THE ORIGINS OF EUROPEAN GARDENS

This may sound exotically peripheral to the West but it is salutary to remember how relatively recent European gardening is compared with that of the great Oriental civilizations. In Europe, the traditions started in ancient Greece, with sacred groves and gardens around shrines, sanctuaries and temples, but in secular gardens the Persian influence was naturally strong as a result of Alexander's expeditions. Although there are no paintings or other delineations of Greek gardens, their literature describes elaborate public and private layouts with statuary, fountains, grottoes, and walks framed with trees and flowerbeds. Funerary gardens developed, too, planted with appropriate subjects like asphodel, acanthus and cypresses, complete with wells, walls, walks and occasionally dining pavilions.

These Hellenistic gardens, along with those of Egypt and Persia, shaped the gardens of ancient Rome. But the Romans, great imitators and adaptors that they were, assimilated them into a new aesthetic and left us detailed written descriptions, many pictorial representations, and in particular the actual garden layouts themselves, either preserved in ruins like that of the Emperor Hadrian, or under volcanic ash, as at Pompeii, Herculaneum and other sites. As a consequence a number of the actual layouts have been restored to near-exact representations of these antique pleasure grounds and parks on the one hand and the courtyards within the house on the other. In these there were many sacred themes, and overall the sense of the garden expressing Nature as a divine presence. The art of European gardens, as we know them, began here.

After the collapse of the Roman Empire, gardening was almost entirely restricted to the confines of castles and monasteries: medieval gardens, essentially small and enclosed, and often fortified. Even when the need for security diminished in the 16th century – the Tudor and Elizabethan period in Britain – gardens remained small, walled and formal. Beds, whether of plants or grass, formed neat patterns before being developed into the fancy knots and larger parterres in which the design, created in low hedging, was more important than the plants. Alleys, tunnels and arbours often formed important features.

CLASSICAL GARDENING TRADITIONS

Renaissance Italians freed themselves of these medievally based enclosures, rapidly developing a very elaborate style of gardening to match their classically styled villas, with formal hedges and topiary, parterres and terraces, grandiose steps, ornaments, statuary, grottoes, and with water everywhere – in fountains, conduits and canal-shaped pools. There is a striking parallelism between Renaissance gardens and contemporary ones of Mughul India, though there was no contact between the two.

This is a characteristic medieval garden which includes a tunnel arbour covered in climbing roses, which were widely grown at the time. It is very much an enclosed retreat from the outside world. It features La Dame au Jardin (15th century) from Le Livre d'Heures d'Antoine de Navarre. (Bodleian Library, Oxford)

This 'lunette' painting of the villa and gardens of Castello by Giusto Utens in the late 16th century depicts the elaborate formal gardens of the Grand Duke Cosimo the Great, laid out in about 1540. Built on a gentle slope it included two giardini segreti, or secret gardens, at each end of the mansion, a planting of dense evergreen trees around a central fountain, a grotto and a tree house. The formally arranged gardens also contained much handsome sculpture – a typical Renaissance feature. (Museo di Firenze Com'era, Florence)

Italian gardens were designed to provide shade and coolness on hot summer days. When the style reached France (after Charles VII's Italian conquest in 1495) and other parts of Europe a little later, the plan became larger in scale and often more open, the garden very much a place for promenading. This was partly because of the terrain; in flat French countryside the hillside cascades of Italy were perforce transformed into canals and pools.

The vastest and most influential garden in France was Versailles where the grandeur of Italian High Renaissance, with its huge quantities of stonework, water effects and statuary, reached its apogee. To quote Julia Berrall (*The Garden*), 'The splendour of Louis XIV's Versailles was the envy of every reigning monarch and prince in Europe. During his reign and the Regency after his death, royal visitors came to be entertained or to follow in the fashionable footsteps of others. "A young man," said Frederick II, "passed for an imbecile if he had not stayed for some time at Versailles." All spent vast sums of money building or enlarging palaces, planning gardens, and hiring architects and designers, in the hope of emulating Louis' achievement.'

The countries adjoining Italy, notably Austria, Switzerland and southern Germany, were influenced more or less directly by its garden style; but most of Europe's gardens were transformed following the most explosive effect of Versailles and the example of its designer Le Nôtre (who had earlier designed Vaux-le-Vicomte which had prompted Louis XIV's megalomaniac efforts at Versailles). These gardens ranged across Europe from Spain and Portugal to Leningrad and Sweden; even the Emperor of China had gardens created in the Renaissance manner.

A particular feature of these European layouts was the extension of vistas within the garden to the surrounding countryside, by planting tree avenues or by cutting vistas through woodland, often with total disregard for the peasantry, whose villages were sometimes removed entirely.

In Holland, the French style was merged with a characteristic native one, in which there are many small beds and divisions, more closely related to the intimate, enclosed, four-parted gardens of the late Middle Ages. The overriding necessity for dykes and canals in the flat, low-lying terrain made it necessary to incorporate these in the design, as at William of Orange's garden at Het Loo. Some German gardens in particular imitated this idea and incorporated canals as part of their design.

BRITISH GARDENING – THE NATURAL LANDSCAPE

There were various divergences from the basic formal landscape theme, notably the rococo, in which Louis XIV's solemn and heavily burdened approach is treated in a lighter, and more light-hearted, manner. Some of these gardens have been preserved in Germany, but in Britain the sojourn of rococo gardening, intrinsically fragile, was brief indeed, and is now almost entirely known from the paintings of Thomas Robins. Here we can see the Chinoiserie and the pasteboard Gothic with its serpentine walks. Chinoiserie, which started at Versailles in 1670, might be called 'Chinese gardening from hearsay'; it was based on travellers' accounts and illustrations of the period and lacked any clear understanding or real conception of its underlying principles.

Nevertheless it may have had some effect on the reaction against formality that struck British gardening next, for, in principle, the Chinese garden has neither symmetry nor formality, being designed to symbolize nature. Although the Chinese garden is typically composed of a multiplicity of enclosed areas, they appear to be arranged at random, and the main enclosure usually has a large, irregularly shaped pool, with buildings around it linked by a meandering path or by sinuous galleries. The traditional, bizarrely formed rocks – such an important feature in the Chinese garden – are also irregular in both their form and positioning.

Though very far from Chinese, the English landscape garden, born in England early in the 18th century, replaced formality and was also a return to naturalness, though in a far less stylized way. Interestingly enough, it was the writer Joseph Addison and the poet Alexander Pope who first expressed dissatisfaction with formality and made natural

This watercolour of the gardens of Drummond Castle was painted in the 19th century by Jacob Thompson, but the terraced garden was originally created in the 17th century and much restored in the mid-19th century. Contemporary writers described it as a mingling of Italian, French and Dutch styles. (Private Collection)

beauty the aim. The theme of the landscape gardens that emerged is summed up in Horace Walpole's inimitable, much-quoted phrases about William Kent: 'He leaped the fence and saw that all nature was a garden . . . the pencil of his imagination bestowed all the arts of landscape on the scenes he handled.'

This return to Arcady, as it has been called, had in fact been presaged by Le Nôtre's informal *bosquets* at Versailles, but was undoubtedly influenced by the paintings of real and imaginary landscapes by the 17th-century painters Claude Lorrain and Gaspard Poussin, by the latter's brother-in-law Nicholas Poussin, and to a lesser extent by the wilder ones of Salvator Rosa. A great number of the paintings of Claude and Gaspard feature the temple of the Sibyl at Tivoli. This became the most often copied building in landscape gardens in Britain and on the Continent, among many copies of typically ancient buildings, primarily those of ancient Italy. Such reconstructions were often part-ruined, to provoke a heightened feeling of antiquity and human transience.

William Kent (1684–1748), the architect and landscape gardener, had been trained as a painter, and developed the inspiration of Claudian landscapes into three-dimensional 'landscape pictures', one following another as the visitor proceeds from one to the next round the garden. The most famous example of this is probably Stourhead, Wiltshire – built by an amateur garden designer, Henry Hoare, from around 1744 onwards – where the landscape pictures are mostly created on a circuit around the garden's central lake, an echo of the 'Grand Tour', when the traveller took a 'viewing glass' with which to frame a particularly attractive view as if it were a painting. Stourhead is also an example of the fashion for a literary background to a landscape, as its landscape pictures are based on episodes in Virgil's *Aeneid*.

The influence of landscape painting, resulting in a style known as the Picturesque, must not be exaggerated: it played a part in shaping designs but a much greater one in influencing current thinking about natural scenery.

As mentioned above, the English landscape style was, in due course, taken up in Europe, a reversal of the way in which formality had reached English shores, though influences came from other quarters as well. On the Continent landscape gardeners experimented more wildly than their British counterparts (sometimes resulting in strange excesses); many examples were known as *jardins anglais*.

All the architecture and associations of the early English landscape gardens were banished in the mature work of the best known landscape gardener, Lancelot 'Capability' Brown (1716–83), who swept away virtually every trace of wall and terrace, parterre and waterworks. His aim, instead, was to emphasize the qualities of natural landscape; he might raise a hill here or create a lake there, remove or plant trees to enhance contours and lines, but he was simply developing what was there. He took the grass of the park right up to the walls of the mansion and seldom placed a new building in the landscape except for the occasional bridge.

Many, including Joshua Reynolds, felt that Brown's gardening, and certainly that of his followers, copied nature too closely for the result to be any form of art, considering that 'Gardening, as far as Gardening is an Art . . . is a deviation from nature.'

Reaction against Brown's smooth effects occurred on a small scale, carried out by devotees of the Picturesque, who continued to create what can be called contrived landscapes, and wrote a number of essays on the subject. There were also one or two vast gardens made around the turn of the 18th century which attempted to emulate wild nature, like William Beckford's Fonthill in Britain and Jean-Joseph de Laborde's Méréville in France.

Parallel with the development of the landscape garden (something for less well-endowed estates) was the concept of the *ferme ornée* or ornamented farm, with ornamental walks in which shrubs, climbers and herbaceous plants were grown, set into a working farm, the livestock being kept away from these promenades by hedges. As the name im-

*Built for the Prince Regent in 1787, the Royal Pavilion, Brighton, and its
grounds, were acquired by Brighton town in 1850. John Nash – who had
been a partner of Humphry Repton – had laid out the grounds,
shrubberies and beds, which were in a vaguely Picturesque style. Although
most of the flowers in this engraving seem to be roses, many exotics were also grown.*

plies, the idea seems to have been basically French, but the English seized upon it with enthusiasm. It was similar to an earlier concept of 'wilderness planting' which had sometimes been related to formal gardens.

THE AMERICAN GARDENING
TRADITION

It is interesting to note that Thomas Jefferson (1743–1826) third President of the United States, made plans after his visit to England in 1786, for his estate at Monticello, Virginia, to include a *ferme ornée* and 'lawns and clumps of Trees, the lawns opening so as to give advantageous catches of prospect.' This seems to be a combination of landscape and farmstead.

There had been two distinct influences on the develop-

ment of North American gardens up to this point. The first European settlers were the Spaniards who founded St Augustine in Florida in 1565. Before the end of that century, there were several Spanish cities along the Florida and Georgia coasts, which the scanty records indicate were filled with many kinds of fruit tree and potherbs, in typically Spanish architectural settings. On the west coast Spaniards created missions from 1697 onwards, and the Californian ones established by Franciscans in 1797 soon became prolific with a large range of fruit and ornamental trees, useful herbs and flowers grown for ornament, forerunners of that state's present lushness in gardening.

The second strand of American gardening began in the much more stringent circumstances of the settlers from Britain, Holland, Sweden and other European countries which started with the landing of the Pilgrim Fathers at

Plymouth, New England, in 1620. Most of these had brought seeds, and vegetable and herb gardens were quickly established. The military in their numerous forts were assiduous growers of fruit and vegetables. For many years personal gardens were of the simplest kind, typically small rectangles with a central path to the house, very like the archetypal English cottage garden; vegetables, herbs and fruit were set off with a gradually increasing number of ornamental plants, many of them the handsome American wild species that grew around.

Of course each group of colonists based their gardens on the design traditions and plant materials of their home-

The grounds at Bowood House were originally laid out by 'Capability' Brown between 1761 and 1768. In the early 19th century two great formal terraces were created by the house, forming the Italian garden seen here with a geometric parterre filled with bedding plants. (Royal Horticultural Society, London)

lands. As more prosperous settlers arrived, the effect became stronger – those from Britain, for instance, designing houses like the great manors at home, with formal, compartmented gardens, and those from Holland using clipped hedges, topiary and beds filled with flowers. In the south the palatial plantation gardens recalled, in their organization, the Roman rural villa described by Pliny and, in their style, the Palladian villas of the Renaissance.

Along the Gulf coast both the climate and the original Spanish architecture encouraged Mediterranean-style gardens and planting, with enclosed patios increasingly used as space became more limited.

THE ADVENT OF SMALLER GARDENS

Back in Britain Capability Brown's death in 1783 was accompanied by a reaction to his ideas, accelerated by social, agricultural and industrial changes in Britain, which in broad terms resulted in the reduction of huge estates. The man who took on Brown's mantle, Humphry Repton (1752–1818), had to rethink the old master's principles. Repton reintroduced the concept of the more formal garden close to the house, including flowerbeds, terraces, shrubberies, gravel walks, trelliswork, loggias and conservatories. The park, where it still existed, was distanced from the house.

Repton, a talented painter, took up landscape design only in 1788. He combined his talents in the famous 'before and after' watercolours of gardens for clients, many of which are considerable works of art themselves.

Repton wrote of his policies how 'The scenery of nature, called landscape, and that of a garden, are as different as their uses: one is to please the eye, the other is for the comfort and occupation of man'. In this way gardens returned to having a social purpose, such as Jane Austen describes so well in *Mansfield Park* and other novels.

After Repton's death in 1818, John Claudius Loudon (1783–1843) became the next chief arbiter of garden design and management at a time when the Industrial Revolution was gaining strength and a new middle class arose, resulting in myriads of gardens in and around the spreading centres of industry. Labour was so cheap that few middle-class families did not own a garden of an acre or more, with greenhouses and a conservatory, while much urban and suburban housing had small gardens.

Loudon adapted Repton's style to these circumstances, in what was essentially a scaled-down version of the Picturesque, with beds both geometric and informal, shrubs and trees informally placed, sometimes grouped in shrubberies, sometimes with rockwork and with statues and ornaments. This trend towards allowing plants to grow as naturally as possible, which Loudon called 'Gardenesque', went beyond small gardens into arboretums and pinetums.

THE NEW TECHNOLOGY AND ITS EFFECTS

On both sides of the Atlantic two factors accelerated gardening change. One was the huge range of novel tools and devices made possible by new technology, among them the invention of the cylinder lawn mower in 1830, which allowed the lawn to become an integral part of virtually every garden layout, large or small. New technology also permitted the development of the greenhouse, as iron replaced wood and masonry. The architectural conservatory slowly gave way to more utilitarian metal structures, although some were elegantly curved, that contained much more glass in proportion to framework than previously.

The second factor was the ever-increasing wealth of new plants as plant hunters explored almost every part of the world. Every type of plant was included – conifers and other trees, shrubs, herbaceous plants, bulbs and their ilk, as well as exotic greenhouse subjects. These introductions meant that the contents of the garden became as important as its design, while the tender subjects filled the new greenhouses and began a fashion for plants indoors, and opened the way to their multiplication in vast numbers, under the new expanse of glass, to provide formal flowerbeds with brilliant patterned colour during the summer months.

These bedding plants found their way into every suburban garden and town park, as well as into the vast formal, Italianate gardens designed to accompany the classically styled villas created by Charles Barry, William Nesmith and others. Tender plants in blocks of brilliant colour were replanted each season in the most labour-intensive form of gardening ever known.

Changes in gardening style took place at different rates in different countries. In Europe, where the Napoleonic Wars had curtailed change, landscape gardening continued till the middle of the 19th century, after which aspects of the Gardenesque and in particular 'bedding out' took over. The French went in for huge beds of one kind of plant only and they also originated sub-tropical bedding, using large plants with variegated or otherwise impressive foliage, nowadays grown only as house plants.

In North America, perhaps as a contrast to the wilderness of the pioneer country, the formality of European late-17th-century gardening persisted till Loudon's Gardenesque was translated by America's first native landscape designer, Alexander Jackson Downing in the 1840s. What he practised with enormous influence was, in part, a return to the Picturesque and in part a more formal landscape which he called 'the Graceful'. The Picturesque garden was to be set off with a Gothic or cottage-style house, the Graceful with a classical villa and its ornamental appurtenances.

After the Civil War (1861–65), America, like Europe,

LEFT: *The Jacobean house of Blickling Hall has had a formal garden since the 17th century. In the 1930s the fussy beds of the Victorian layout were simplified by Norah Lindsay, a well-known designer of the time, who made several one-colour beds in grass with long borders on either side, retaining the existing yew hedges and clipped topiary. This border, painted by Beatrice Parsons (1870-1955) displays the exuberance of vividly coloured perennials, set off by the impressive façade of the mansion behind. (Christopher Wood Gallery, London)*

RIGHT: *This late-Impressionist American painting, entitled 'Open Air Breakfast' by William Merritt Chase shows the forerunner of the modern 'outdoor room', an enclosed garden used primarily for social activities and recreation, rather than for serious gardening. (Toledo Museum of Art)*

became more industrialized. Gardens were more complex and cluttered with ornament, their design derived from many sources. But the newly rich industrial magnates creating their opulent mansions and gardens looked back to the European past.

It is interesting to note very similar tastes in Australia, just a little earlier than in America. Later in the 19th century, the Victorian trends for the Gardenesque, soon coupled with the taste for bedding out, prevailed, as indeed they did in New Zealand.

CHANGING FASHIONS

Gardening is prone to suffer huge changes of fashion. The appetite for bedding out was eventually undermined by rising costs and by adverse reaction from several writers and editors, notably Shirley Hibberd. The loudest fulminations came from the gardener and garden writer William Robinson (1838-1935). He had been impressed, on a visit to Paris in 1867, by the bedding schemes – which the French carried out quite as assiduously as the British – and wrote of how the temporary plants in these borders were mixed with 'permanent things – lilac bushes, roses, etc. which give a line of verdure throughout the centre of the border, and prevent it from being quite overdone with flowers.'

Returning home he began to campaign vigorously for a return to more naturalistic gardening with permanent hardy plants, and to 'wild' gardening. This, wrote Robinson, 'is applied essentially to the placing of perfectly hardy exotic plants under conditions where they will thrive without further care'. Sub-tropical bedding was replaced by the use of hardy plants which still had a tropical appearance, like acanthus, bamboos, fatsia and yuccas, and were of course planted permanently.

Robinson was abetted by Gertrude Jekyll (1843-1932), who turned her painter's eye to the design of herbaceous borders with carefully planned colour associations. She

I have already mentioned the ever-increasing number of new plant introductions, now increasingly combined with breeding of new varieties. Gertrude Jekyll made an interesting comment: 'One modern French artist has described painting as *l'art des sacrifices* . . . the best free gardening is also an art demanding constant restraint and a constant sacrifice.'

The British have always been notably addicted to new and rare plants for their own sake, and some 20th century gardens fail to show the recommended restraint; instead, they are full of plants grown as individuals without any special thought given to their artistic association. Such 'plantsmanship' has given rise to gardens of specialized plants, for instance of one genus like the iris, one type of plant like the alpine, or one special aim like flower arranging.

In Brazil, Roberto Burle Marx pioneered a style in which large groups of one plant formed free-flowing patterns among pools and often decorative paths, which has been followed by designers in various countries, including Australia. Many British gardens are naturalistic woodlands which may be said to display a long-standing vein of romanticism.

These days, the styles of the past are often emulated; features like knots and arbours are sometimes recreated, and 'period' ornaments are widely used. Like so much else in the world, in this epoch of instant communication and widespread of information, garden designers meld together all that they find best in the past, while developing their own personal styles. Different countries do have distinct preferences for different plants; for instance rhododendrons in Britain, North America and New Zealand, and conifers in Germany and Scandinavia. These choices tend to be influenced by climate, like the cactus gardens in California and the sub-tropical gardens in the south of France (a great many of which, incidentally, were laid out by English garden designers).

In smaller gardens there is a trend towards paving and

would probably never have given up painting for garden design had she not developed severe myopia while relatively young. It was her painter's eye, without doubt, which enabled her to create the most detailed garden compositions with such a sense of colour harmony. Explaining how gardening is made a fine art, she wrote that the secret was 'to place every plant or group of plants with such thoughtful care and definite intention that they shall form part of a harmonious whole, and that successive portions, or in some cases even single details, shall show a series of pictures'.

Working in partnership with the architect Edwin Lutyens, Gertrude Jekyll also stood for unity in style between house and garden, one of the tenets of the Arts and Crafts movement inspired by John Ruskin and William Morris. The movement also encouraged enthusiasm for old-fashioned flowers and the revival of the cottage garden. In permitting styles to be mingled, it led to the most seminal garden of the 20th century, Lawrence Johnston's Hidcote Manor, with its layout of many self-contained units.

The importance here of Ruskin, Morris and Jekyll is another example of two-way influences between gardening and painting.

LEFT: These colourful double borders, painted by Lilian Stannard, are crowded with late summer colour in the shape of dahlias, Michaelmas daisies, hollyhocks and sunflowers. In the late 19th and early 20th century, such large herbaceous borders were the showpiece of many large gardens, but few could afford the labour needed to maintain them successfully today. (Private Collection)

RIGHT: This 'Dream Garden' by David Suff, painted in 1987 and exhibited in the Royal Academy Summer Exhibition in London, is, as the artist has explained, not so much the garden of the artist's aspirations as one in which dreams can be dreamed. The dark setting of the clipped hedges and topiary is formal, but the architecturally grouped herbaceous plants, setting off their texture and form, give a thoroughly modern feel to the garden. (Private Collection)

architectural features and many modern small gardens are now very much controlled works of art, with plants carefully selected for shape and texture, and materials like paving, brick, cobbles, concrete features, raised platforms and small pools chosen as a deliberate contrast to the leaf forms.

In an increasingly harsh and competitive world, gardens these days, whether large or small, are more than ever sanctuaries for their owners and we come back to the antique conception of the garden as a paradise, in which we, the gardeners, alter our surroundings to create something uniquely our own.

A garden changes with the seasons, and it develops, matures, and finally often decays; Mac Griswold calls it 'the slowest of the performing arts'. A painting records a moment in time.

AUTHOR'S NOTE:

Although this book was not conceived as a history of gardening, it has been arranged in periods, with the Oriental examples as a separate chapter.

Many artists have depicted gardens and this book cannot represent them all. Several quite famous ones have not found a place, but all the major schools of painting have been included.

In commenting on the 60 paintings reproduced in this book, I have picked on different aspects of gardening according to the type of garden depicted, which are often so disparate. I have done my best to identify the plants being grown, or suggested modern-day alternatives, and indicated, where feasible, ways in which the garden, or part of it, could inspire something in a similar vein.

A short list of the plants available at the times discussed is given on pages 156-7.

Pliny the Elder: Historia Naturalis Sienese, c. 1460. London, Victoria and Albert Museum

CHAPTER ONE

THE

ENCLOSED

GARDEN

Gardens from Roman times to the

end of the medieval period

EMPRESS LIVIA'S GARDEN ROOM

Roman wall painting

ROME (MUSÉE DES THERMES)

The ancient Romans, great agriculturists as they became, developed gardening alongside agriculture as an important adjunct of daily life, and at various levels, from the imperial palace garden to the scholarly retreat. The agricultural writers Columella and Varro, particularly the latter, have left us descriptions of contemporary gardening; Pliny the Younger described his own villa, and others give us glimpses of Roman horticulture in their writings. Many Roman gardens have been excavated and analysed, and several of them have actually been reconstructed and replanted on the same lines as the originals, notably at Pompeii.

There are also pictorial representations of garden scenes, one of the best known being this *trompe-l'oeil* fresco in the Empress Livia's villa by the Prima Porte of ancient Rome. The fresco, of which the scene shown here is only a part, ran around all four walls of a subterranean 'garden' room, which provided a cool haven on hot summer days. In Pliny's Tuscan villa, the garden room had a central fountain, cooling and murmurous, and one can surmise the same here, in Livia's sanctum.

In the foreground a simple wooden trellis opens onto a grassed walk beyond which a more solid-looking boundary with three repeated patterns on its rectangular panels – of wood, or possibly stone – separates garden from shrubs and trees. A few small herbaceous plants grow at regular intervals along this walk, while the embrasure in the further fence frames an oak tree. Elsewhere in the fresco a fruiting pomegranate and an apple tree echo the oranges, and by the fence there are wild flowers – orange and white ox-eye daisies and what looks like a poppy. The pinkish blooms are roses, flowers greatly prized by the Romans, who had many scores of different varieties; the petals were used for strewing floors during banquets.

Several 'funeral' cypresses, *Cupressus sempervirens,* fill in the background of this bosky landscape, just as today the same eastern Mediterranean trees fill the Italian landscape and its gardens. Their presence suggests that parkland lies beyond the imaginary garden of the fresco, and distant mountains can be seen in other parts of the painting. The scene is full of birds of many kinds, including a pair in a birdcage on the fence.

A scene like this could be recreated in a larger garden by making a rectangular plot in an area of shrubs and trees, perhaps either grassed or paved, and with fences around it and a fountain or other ornament in the centre. A garden pavilion could be used as a substitute for the Roman 'garden' room.

A MEDIEVAL HERB GARDEN

Anon, late 14th century

LONDON (BRITISH LIBRARY)

This is a classic illustration, showing us without any artistic licence what a certain sort of medieval garden looked like. It is a French illustration to one of the many versions and translations of the influential *Opus ruralium . . . commodorum*, the source book for gardening and agricultural writers for over two centuries, and completed about 1305 by the Italian Petrus de Crescentiis, often known as Crescentius.

The square plots with paths between them are typical of medieval gardens. Some were just of grass, but others held ornamental plants which might be supported on an elaborate metal or wooden framework (see page 9). Others, as here, were kitchen gardens containing vegetables and culinary herbs. This is a herbalist's town garden, devoted mostly to medicinal herbs, and the square beds greatly simplify both cultivation and harvesting. Like every garden of its time, this one was enclosed by a wall; it could be reached directly from the dwelling in the background, and access to the street beyond was provided by a gate – which would normally be kept firmly locked. The herbalist is directing his head gardener (in a blue jerkin), while other gardeners tend and gather herbs.

It is very difficult to identify the plants shown with certainty. The head gardener is bending over a bed of blue columbine *(Aquilegia)* which was used as a sedative and an antiseptic. Behind the woman at the bottom right are plants of mullein – used for relieving bruises and also as a sedative – and fennel, primarily a culinary herb, good for the digestion. There are some larger plants, seen on the left and in a longer bed at the back, which look like cabbages or, to be more precise for the period, the loose-leaved cole-wort that was the cabbage's ancestor.

A great many other medicinal plants, such as hyssop, feverfew, horehound and clary sage, were grown, and some of these, plus lily, iris, violet and peony, were both medicinal and ornamental. Most of the food-enhancing herbs grown in kitchen gardens had strong flavours, like the fennel already mentioned, the seed of which was much used.

Most modern herb gardens are either informal or arranged in rather more florid patterns than these simple squares, and often edged with box or cotton lavender or set out like a knot bed. The idea of this particular garden, however, has been copied here and there. One of the easiest ways to achieve the effect is to alternate square paving stones with similar-sized squares of open soil in which the individual plants are grown, creating an attractive checkerboard pattern enlivened by the leaves and flowers of the herbs. In this way there is easy access to the plants.

A small herb garden could accommodate a dozen useful culinary herbs – parsley, dill, mint, sage, thyme, rosemary, garlic, chives, coriander, hyssop, winter savory and chamomile – in a neat arrangement of stone slabs and beds.

THE GARDEN OF PARADISE

Überrheinischer Meister, c. 1410-20

FRANKFURT (STÄDELSCHES KUNSTINSTITUT)

This brilliant painting by an unknown Rhenish artist shows, superficially, what a medieval garden within castle walls might be like. Most of it is a 'flowery mead' (as discussed in a simpler painting on page 33) with wild flowers growing luxuriantly in the grass. Behind there is a raised bed formed of wooden planks; a marble table and a well complete the furniture.

This Paradise Garden, or Mary Garden as it is sometimes called, not only reflects the garden practices of the period but is filled with Christian symbolism. It is a *hortus conclusus*, an enclosed garden, in which the Virgin Mary sits on a vast cushion with the infant Jesus at her feet playing with a psaltery held by St Cecilia. Cherries are being picked from the Tree of Life by St Dorothy, water is being scooped up by St Martha. St Michael, winged, sits on the right, with his subdued demon in ape-like form by his feet. St George, telling the story of the infancy of Jesus, sits in front of him,

and in the foreground is the slain Dragon. The pensive young man by the fruitless tree – The Tree of Death – is probably a knight who died prematurely, to whom the painting is a memorial.

The plants so accurately portrayed are also full of symbolism. The white lilies – later called Madonna lilies – represent Mary's purity, while the lilies of the valley represent both purity and meekness. The iris, royally connected, suggests Jesus's descent from the house of David. Red roses stand for divine love and the cherry for the joys of heaven. Strawberries are the fruits of righteousness, and their three-parted leaves symbolize the Trinity, while periwinkle wards off evil.

In the foreground the grafted olive recalls St Paul's parable on 'graffing' contained in his Epistle to the Romans; its lack of fruit may also symbolize the young knight's unfulfilled life.

The plants depicted are as follows: from the well and by the wall, left to right: cowslip; daisy; rose; cherry tree; germander speedwell (Veronica chamaedrys); balm (Melissa officinalis); probably Lychnis chalcedonica; sweet rocket (Hesperis matronalis); flag iris; hollyhocks; Madonna lily (Lilium candidum); yellow wallflower cowslip; columbine (aquilegia). Foreground, left to right: brooklime (Veronica beccabunga); lily-of-the-valley (Convallaria majalis); peony (Paeonia mascula); periwinkle (Vinca minor); sweet violet (above Vinca). Centre: spring snowflake (Leucojum vernum); strawberry in flower and fruit.

EMILIA IN HER GARDEN

from 'Master of the Hours of Burgundy', c. 1465

VIENNA (ÖSTERREICHISCHE NATIONALBIBLIOTHEK)

The medieval word *herber*, from the Latin *herbarium*, does not necessarily mean a herb garden, though it does sometimes refer to one for medicinal herbs only. The word really describes a small, specialized plot with a lawn and very often flowers for decoration. This illustration, from a French manuscript, is the most detailed that exists of this type of garden. The lady sits on a turf bench; trellis behind her supports double climbing roses, and further roses grow on each side of the archway in the background. The roses are *Rosa gallica*, the Red Rose of Lancaster, from which most of our garden roses grown ever since have evolved, and *R. alba*, the White Rose of York, in its form *maxima*.

Between the trellis on the left and the castle wall lies the entrance to a tunnel arbour, on which vines are growing. This seems to be continued behind the archway, where there is a castellated masonry wall behind. Through the archway, in a raised bed created by a low wall in front of the tall one, there is an iris plant and presumably more low flowering plants on each side. More border flowers are planted in the foreground and the low, squared railing is set against another raised bed of bricks, which holds carnations and pinks. In front of the diamond-pattern railing at the bottom of the painting are columbines, a hollyhock, an unidentifiable low plant, stocks, probably French lavender *(Lavandula stoechas)* – which was then called stockadove –

and on the right, probably, rosemary.

It is interesting to see what a number of apparently modern gardening ideas are gathered together here. Trellis is still very much in fashion, though archways are usually simpler affairs these days.

The raised beds are also similar to those seen today. Such beds need to be at least 12in (30cm) wide and 12in (30cm) deep to prevent the soil drying out too quickly; they are perfect for rock plants and spring-flowering bulbs lifted to make way for summer bedding plants.

The turf seat, though seldom seen today, was a very common feature of early gardens. Many medieval garden illustrations, of course, come from parts of Europe where the summers were warm and dry, but even so one cannot avoid the thought that the turf must often have been rather damp to sit on, and cushions are very seldom suggested! In spite of this drawback, however, a turf seat or a turfed bank can look unusual and appealing in the right sort of garden, especially if made with a fragrant plant like thyme or chamomile which needs no clipping. A stone slab set flush with the greenery would reduce the problem of dampness.

Every part of this garden could easily be recreated in a present-day one, since trellis is readily available, and there are some florid archway designs to be found. The garden could either be just as it is in the picture, in a small walled 'patio', or could form a garden room within a larger area.

A turf bench, with a brick base, with a slab of stone in the centre to provide a seat

SCENE IN A GARDEN

from 'Le Romaunt de la Rose', c. 1485

LONDON (BRITISH LIBRARY)

Written in the early part of the 13th century, the *Romaunt de la Rose* by the Frenchman, Guillaume de Lorris, establishes the traditional medieval way of writing about gardens, just as it establishes the pleasures and conventions of courtly love. This famous poem, later translated by Chaucer, is in fact a heavily disguised allegory of the Fall of Man, of man in the enclosed garden which, like all earthly gardens, must wither at summer's end.

Here we see the lover, in blue, looking demure and perhaps a trifle apprehensive, first seeking admission to the portal of the castellated, enclosed garden. He then walks up a path of chamomile, which releases its scent underfoot, towards the arched gateway beyond, where his beloved apparently awaits; there is music, and there will be dancing and other pleasures.

The roses of the title – all white in this illustration – cover the trellis in the background. In the original of this sumptuous 15th-century manuscript version of the poem, a red semi-double rose, with a pink and a small pansy, forms part of the marginal decoration. Roses were very important in medieval gardens, as can be see in the painting of Emilia's garden shown on the preceding page.

This garden has a number of interesting features. The area on the right is of gravel, or perhaps just earth, with two raised beds whose sides, apparently formed of stone slabs, are interestingly sloped. The left-hand division, where the action is, has daisy-spangled grass; the musicians must be sitting on a raised grass seat. The fountain is extremely elaborate for the time; apparently made of metal, its several spouts pour water into a circular stone basin, from which surplus water drains via a channel through a protected archway to beyond the wall.

The space has been divided into two distinct gardens: a practice reintroduced in the 20th century by the American, Lawrence Johnston, at Hidcote Manor, his famous Gloucestershire garden, and copied by Vita Sackville-West at Sissinghurst Castle, Kent. As with the Chinese, who divide small spaces into even tinier ones to make the whole seem more extensive, this is a very useful way to foreshorten the long narrow plots typical of town and suburban gardens today, with divisions of fencing, hedges or fruit trees.

The close-woven trellis-work set in wooden framing, dividing one garden from another, is very characteristic of the Middle Ages but could easily be copied today.

Trellis, wattle and picket fences can all be used to enclose a garden, or part of it, and provide excellent support for climbers like roses or clematis

MEDIEVAL COURTYARD GARDEN

from a French manuscript, 15th century

PARIS (BIBLIOTHÈQUE NATIONALE)

This charming manuscript rendering of a man declaiming – or possibly singing – in a courtyard is interesting historically as well as horticulturally. In Europe during the 12th and 13th centuries monasteries were the main centres for gardeners and gardens, since the aristocracy spent much of their time fighting each other and peasants were too poverty-stricken to contemplate growing anything they could not eat. But during the 13th century, as wars became less frequent, an interest in gardening grew up outside the monastic cloisters. Illustrated on page 31 is a medieval town garden, and this one, somewhat earlier, shows a small garden within a castellated wall. Defences were still essential, and no one ventured to lay out any estate outside the castle, so gardening took place within its walls. Grass plots were made from turf collected in the countryside. Being native turf, it still had wild flowers in it and thus the concept of the 'flowery mead', in which not only wild but deliberately planted flowers would flourish, developed.

This stylized scene is interesting because the flowers are not only in the turf but in containers as well and the urns are unusually elaborate for the period. The white flowers are white campion *(Silene alba)* rendered here with four petals instead of five, but unmistakable with their inflated calyces. The blue on the left is lesser periwinkle *(Vinca minor)* and the red in the foreground comes from a carnation (distinguished by its frilled edges). Introduced from Italy, Spain and North Africa, probably by the Normans, carnations became very popular, as other paintings of the general period frequently show. The flower at the man's right foot is probably germander speedwell *(Veronica chamaedrys)* and that by his left is the scarlet pimpernel *(Anagallis arvensis).*

Except for the carnation, these are native plants. White campion seems to have no uses, but periwinkle had a number of herbal applications as well as folklore associations.

There is not enough here to attempt a reproduction in a modern garden, but the idea of growing wild flowers in grass has become popular recently on both sides of the Atlantic. There are purveyors of wild flower seeds to enable you to create your own flowery mead, though this is not as easy as it may sound.

The concept of natural gardening in grass has an older beginning in the 'alpine meadow', usually made up of bulbous plants like narcissi, fritillaries, snowdrops and tulip species, and wild plants will often develop in the uncut grass. One successful planting of this type, at Great Dixter, Northiam, Kent, continues its display with Queen Anne's Lace, or cow parsley, and buttercups, the grass being cut only when these are over.

Some splendid swards of wild narcissi, notably the 'hooppetticoat' *(Narcissus bulbocodium)* have been made in various English gardens such as Wisley and the Savill Garden at Windsor. If left to themselves after scattering seed, a dense cover will be achieved after about five years, and will go from strength to strength thereafter.

Vertumne and Pomone, Govaerts. Paris, Louvre

CHAPTER TWO

THE
CLASSICAL
INFLUENCE

Post-Renaissance gardens from

the early 16th century to the late

17th century

SPRING

Abel Grimmer, 16th century

LILLE (MUSÉE DES BEAUX ARTS)

This well known painting closely resembles one by Pieter Brueghel II showing the same scene, and was probably copied from this, since it only shows a section of the Brueghel version. It is very interesting historically, for it shows a transitional stage in the formation of plant beds in European gardens. Medieval gardens, like that on page 25, were often made of small square beds set among paths, forming a chessboard pattern, and for decoration simple shapes of grass between paths were used.

By the 15th century herbal and apparently decorative plants also were being grown in rectangular raised beds, edged with wooden planks, stone slabs or bricks laid flat. From these, as we can see here, beds of more interesting shapes and in more complex patterns evolved. The edgings here are probably formed of bricks, covered with a very hard stucco plaster trowelled to a smooth finish.

What we have here is essentially a primitive parterre, where the pattern of the beds is almost as important as their contents. The numerous gardeners are busy planting them up; some beds already contain tulips, those favourite Dutch flowers. Tulips had reached Holland in 1562, from Turkey via Germany, and became a passion with the Dutch, culminating in the extravagant tulipomania described on page 40. The tulips in this painting and the Brueghel version are in a few colours only, giving no idea of the rainbow possibilities which the breeders soon achieved.

On the right we see gardeners trimming vine plants, whose new young growths will be trained to form a canopy over the sturdy wooden tunnel arbour with its amusing statuesque pilasters at the end.

It would be easy to reproduce such a scheme today, perhaps as a period piece. Raised beds are quite often made, usually constructed with stone walls; many gardeners, however, do use rectangular wooden edgings. The best material is old railway sleepers which, being impregnated with preservative, are extremely long-lasting. These are usually laid two or three deep to create a deep, easily draining bed which can be filled with special soil mixtures depending on the plants to be grown – light and gritty for alpines or dry-loving Mediterranean plants, or peaty for those choice woodlanders and specialized alpines needing just such a root run.

Raised beds can be created from a couple of rows of bricks or from stout wooden planks nailed together

FEAST IN THE PARK OF THE DUKE OF MANTUA

Sebastien Vrancz, c. 1610

ROUEN (MUSÉE DES BEAUX ARTS)

The Duke of Mantua, as befitted his status, had a magnificent mansion, and in front of it, lined up with the house front, there was a formal garden which is very much of its time. Its most prominent feature is the elaborate wood-framed arbour, derived perhaps from the Roman *porticus*, which was basically a shelter from inclement weather. On this, plants are trained and trimmed to form leafy walls, but it is impossible to know what they are – jasmine, rosemary, juniper and roses were among those used at the time.

In those days very few low decorative plants were grown, and the variously shaped and patterned beds with paths around them are made with grass; the knot beds so popular a century earlier were beginning to go out of favour.

On both sides of the grass beds there are low hedges, and the front of the formal area has a wooden paling fence with nicely shaped uprights. A curious feature seen on the right is a narrow canal below the level of both the formal garden and the colonnaded pavilion at the right; on it a gondola is being poled along, and the couple in it are standing up to peer over the fence at the garden.

In some of the grass beds a few small trees are planted, and a couple of Madonna lilies can be discerned, but otherwise the flowering plants are carnations, all growing in pots. The Romans found the carnation growing in Spain, where it was used to flavour drinks, and from late medieval times it became popular again all over Europe.

The pots are earthenware, and each one has a prefabricated wood or metal support to prevent the long brittle carnation stems breaking. Such supports seem to have vanished from gardens after the 16th century, only to reappear in Victorian times and again today.

More flowers can be seen on the wall to the left of the painting, but curiously, these seem to be cut blooms in vases. It is difficult to make most of them out, but an iris is prominent, together with more carnations and a cornflower.

A modern arbour is usually a smallish garden building, often just an open decorative framework; our equivalents of the Renaissance arbour are either the tunnel or the much more open pergola. Tunnels are either made entirely of trained trees or – more often – trees such as laburnum or climbing plants like roses grown on large metal hoops. The pergola, usually rectangular with uprights, crossbars and longitudinal runners, is also used for climbers, wisteria, roses, clematis and ornamental-leaved vines being among the favourites. However, trelliswork arbours very similar to this 16th-century example can occasionally be seen, as in Manet's garden, illustrated on page 99.

Knot gardens and parterres, in which plants play an important part, have been copied in modern times more frequently than the simple patterned grass beds seen here, but such shaped beds, with paving in between, could in fact be very unusual and effective in a highly formal garden.

*Low-growing plants – turf, chamomile or
thyme, set in squares in a brick surround*

RUBENS AND HIS WIFE IN THEIR GARDEN AT ANTWERP

Peter Paul Rubens c. 1632

MUNICH (ALTE PINAKOTHEK)

After his second marriage in 1630, to the 16-year-old Hélène Fourment, Rubens reflected much more of his domestic life in his paintings than he had hitherto. In this scene the couple are strolling in a garden of some size and formality, though the presence of turkeys and quails as well as the proud peacock suggests that the domestic back yard is not far away.

Some typical features of European gardens of the time are prominent here, notably the ornate pavilion housing statues and a bust. Behind, a formal garden is sketched in beyond a low hedge, with a boy-on-a-dolphin fountain in the centre.

The major interest in gardening terms, however, lies in the rectangular plot glimpsed behind the wooden gate, for it is full of tulips and also, apparently, irises. This is, of course, Holland, and the picture must have been painted just when Dutch tulipomania was at its height. Tulips had reached Holland in 1562 from Turkey, where they had long been a cult, and gradually the cultivation and breeding of these became a national obsession. Between 1634 and 1637 this reached absurd levels, and rare varieties, especially new seedlings, changed hands for astronomical sums.

It was at this time, however, that the main groups of tulips used in present-day gardens took shape, though the 'broken' varieties, with flowers striped or streaked in different colours, the most popular of all in 17th-century Holland, are now little grown.

The tulips in the painting seem to be growing in much denser shade than they like, as there are trees right among them as well as overhanging.

The irises may be early kinds of the familiar bearded group growing from horizontal rhizomes, collectively known as *Iris germanica*, a flower cultivated since ancient times whose wild ancestors cannot be established. But since the prominent sword-shaped foliage of this bearded group is not to be seen we cannot be sure; it is perhaps more likely that the flowers are what we now call Spanish and English bulbous irises, native to Europe, with much lighter leaves.

In front of the tulip enclosure there are some orange and lemon trees in pots, brought out from their conservatory according to the widespread practice at the time (see page 57). And right in the foreground two further pots, containing perhaps carnations, hold wood or wicker plant supports of the type widely used in gardens in medieval times. The way Rubens has faithfully depicted the broken support on the right leads one to think that the painting is an actual garden scene, not an imaginary or idealized one.

Nowadays tulips are often massed in beds in parks. In the smaller garden the best effects are often achieved by planting tulips in large containers which can be moved when the plants are in flower to provide an arresting focal point in the garden. Tulips look best in groups of one colour, and for containers the more recent hybrids listed as 'botanical tulips' being mostly short-stemmed and brilliantly coloured, are the most attractive. I wonder what the Dutch tulipomaniacs would have made of them?

GARDEN AT IDSTEIN

Johann Walther, 1650

The parterre (also illustrated and described on page 52) was normally a fairly close pattern of edgings such as dwarf box, cotton lavender and the like but it also developed into symmetrical patterns of small beds filled with plants. This example is very unusual, for the beds are shaped like fruits and leaves. As with all parterres, to get the full impact, it is ideally viewed from a vantage point above ground level.

This painting is the frontispiece to the two-volume work in which Johann Walther described and extolled the botanical collection of his patron Johann of Nassau (presumably it is he, with wife and child, in the foreground) at Idstein, near Frankfurt-am-Main.

It is late spring, for the beds are sparsely planted – as was common practice then – with bulbs, mainly tulips and crown imperials *(Fritillaria imperialis)*. In the foreground are various shrubs and a leafy plant, perhaps a yucca; and there are more, doubtless unusual, plants in tubs and pots: on the low wall that subdivides the enclosed garden further back; on the boundary wall at the left; and (though one cannot make them out clearly) on each side of the arched construction in the middle of this wall.

This latter was, in fact, a grotto, topped with a vertical sundial in a sort of belfry, with carvings on an inner arch framing a centrepiece. In this a female figure stood on a stone shell, in an embrasure formed of decorated stonework. All this we know from another of Walther's paintings which also shows plants in pots on three levels set out on either side of the grotto.

On the opposite side to the grotto is an elaborate ornament of a different kind, a wall with high arched entrances and a series of large niches standing individually on top of it along its length.

Knots and parterre gardens have been maintained and also re-created in modern times and it would be amusing to make a garden of fruit shapes like this. It would, of course, involve a similar outlay of work and maintenance of the clipped edgings of dwarf plants. The shapes could be filled with spring bulbs, followed by bedding plants. Or, to emulate Johann of Nassau in his collecting of special plants, each bed could contain a group of plants of one family or genus, or of one type like grey- or golden-leaved kinds.

Such a garden needs formal enclosure, whether with walls, hedges or fences. Alternatively you could make a trellised arched walk or a rectangular pergola all around, on which wisteria, roses or other climbers could be trained. Perhaps apples or pears would be most appropriate to the fruit shapes in the parterre. They could be trained as elongated cordons over metal hoops, or a fruiting grapevine could be grown instead.

PROSPECT OF THE HOUSE AND GARDENS AT LLANERCH

Anon, c. 1662

(PRIVATE COLLECTION)

*T*his is an astonishing garden view for several reasons. It is the first bird's-eye painting of its kind in British art and, as John Harris has pointed out in *The Artist and the Country House*: 'the only fully detailed view of the formal garden of a squire laid out before 1666'. It was indeed built by a squire – one Mutton Davies – named after his maternal grandfather, Sir Peter Mutton.

Llanerch is in a wild part of Wales, but an awkward locality and, perhaps, difficulty of access were easily overcome with adequate wealth. Sadly to relate, it was entirely swept away in the late 18th century by a landscaper following in 'Capability' Brown's footsteps.

The garden in 1662 was Italianate in design; Mutton Davies had spent four years in Italy before he married and his travels clearly influenced the layout of the garden, carried out shortly after his return. Joseph Addison described it later as 'in the foreign taste, with images and water tricks'. It descends in terraces down a slope from the house (which probably dates back to the late 16th century).

The three-level terracing follows the advice of the influential garden writer William Lawson, in his *A New Orchard and Garden* of 1597. Brick and stone walls support and enclose the terraces, embellished with ornate stairways and pavilions; the staircase at upper left conceals a grotto below. The urns on the terrace walls, well filled with colourful flowers, make a nice finishing touch.

Further stairways lead down to steep-sloping tree plantations, between which a broad grass walk descends to a circular water theatre, embellished with upright trees – perhaps cypresses, the centrepoint being a fountain on which stands a statue of Neptune.

The water effects are presumably fed by the river which starts somewhere in the higher ground at the right. An underground conduit probably takes water to the building at the bottom right of the garden, where pumps feed the stepped cascade that emerges from an arched stonework grotto above the building. Tanks there provide a gravity feed to the Neptune fountain and its circular pool, and the water finally leaves the grounds, to rejoin the river, along the canal at the bottom on the left, which provides another walk.

But this is not all the garden has to offer, for to the right of the water theatre an ornate bridge leads out of the garden, perhaps to a wild and shady grove, the 'wilderness', so popular at the time.

Terracing on any scale is very expensive, but is often the best solution to gardening successfully on sloping ground. Most effective on the grand scale (and there are many examples of grand terraces in Europe and in North America), it is equally attractive in smaller sloping gardens.

DENHAM PLACE, BUCKINGHAMSHIRE

British School, c. 1695

NEW HAVEN (YALE CENTER FOR BRITISH ART)

This painting of the late Restoration period is one of many such records of notable houses that were built or adapted around this time, in which artists cleverly portrayed properties from an imagined aerial viewpoint. Denham Place was built by Sir Roger Hill, to designs by William Stanton, between 1688 and 1701, replacing an older mansion which itself had been altered from a Tudor original. Although the painting is in rather primitive style, it is a masterpiece of accurate depiction.

The layout of the gardens is fascinating in many ways, though fairly typical of its time in all respects except for the large numbers of sculptures in it – 44 in all, plus 15 busts and six urns – forming a unique collection for English gardens. Among these there is, on the wall in the centre of the painting, a truly fantastical array of statues of dancing boys, 24 of them in all sorts of poses, and another four on the pillars of the yard entrance, framed with white obelisks.

Although the statues are unusual, the variously shaped grass parterres of the left-hand part of the garden are unremarkable compared with the elaborate designs of other contemporary gardens. More original, however, is the central, diamond-patterned layout of paths and narrow conifers, and the five plots at the right of the picture enclosed by narrow hedges. These were probably planted with young trees to produce an eventual effect like the four rectangular plots at the bottom right of the painting where the trees are starting to mature.

Water features prominently, as in many contemporary gardens. A local river is canalized in the centre and presumably feeds the rectangular pools at right. The elaborate water pavilion in mid-canal is very unusual, but there are no fountains.

Another very interesting aspect of this estate is the tree planting on the left. Avenues of trees figured in many gardens of the kind, but in this one both conifers and deciduous trees have been planted in differently spaced avenues, striding in parallel across a wide expanse of walled parkland.

The component parts of this peculiar garden, seemingly adapted without proper understanding from current European tradition, shows a remarkable lack of cohesion, apart from the parterres in front of and behind the mansion.

Although people often figure in record paintings of this kind, this view of Denham Place is specially enhanced by the depiction of the farmyard in the centre foreground, with its load of hay, cattle, penned sheep and odds and ends lying around.

The house survives today, but the strange formal gardens were a casualty of the 18th-century landscapers; of the statuary only some busts remain, together with a few capitals from the water pavilion. Something similar could easily be created in an urban garden with an interesting display of statuary, set on paving, and with a backdrop of dark evergreens to set off their different forms.

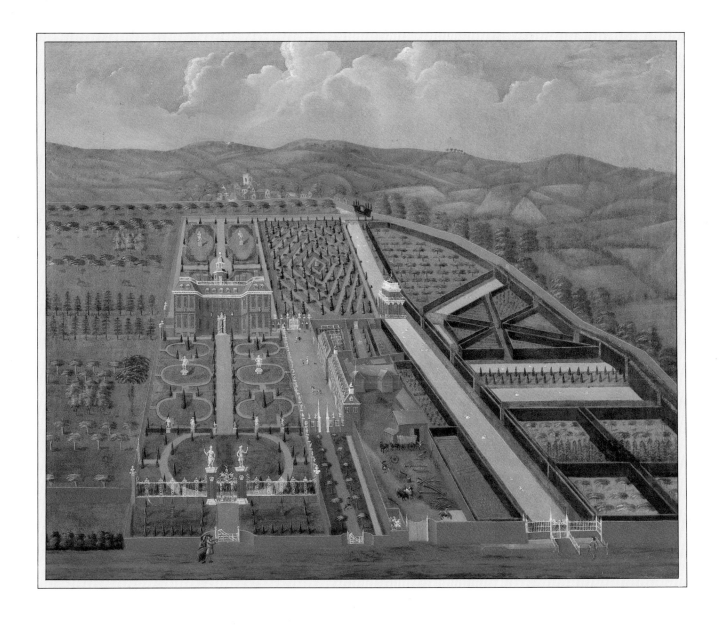

GALERIE DES ANTIQUES AT VERSAILLES

Jean Cotelle, 17th century

Though this gouache is entitled *La Galerie des Antiques* the subject is, in all probability, a *bosquet* made at Versailles between 1680 and 1683, variously known as *La Salle des Antiques* or *La Galerie d'Eau*.

A *bosquet* was basically an ornamental grove or thicket, but the trees around could enclose almost any feature including set-pieces like this one. This particular *salle* was one of the last of many elaborate spectacles created at Versailles by Louis XIV until he began to tire of them. It was replaced in 1704 by the *Salle des Marroniers*, which was simply a lawn surrounded by chestnut trees. (Many of the Versailles *bosquets* were replaced in this way, the statues sometimes moved several times from place to place.)

The classical figures lined up between the fountains are, of course, 'Les Antiques'. The overall design is simple enough: an array of statues punctuated by sets of triple jets of water. In front, rows of trees immaculately clipped into ball shapes rise on ramrod-straight trunks from oblong shapes that are almost certainly of clipped box.

Two formal pools lie across the vista that terminates in a sort of shaped proscenium, with a central statue and fountain, other water jets and more clipped trees. By Versailles standards it is almost humble, one of innumerable tableaux, mostly based on pools and fountains, which the King's visitors were directed to see in a particular order, a tour which would take a day if fully carried out.

As the fountains became more numerous, the problems of finding water and getting it to the flattish site at Versailles increased. Between 1682 and 1684, in an astonishing feat of engineering, and at a cost of over 3 million *livres*, water was raised from the Seine to the required 162 metres. It consisted of 14 enormous waterwheels jutting out into the river, powering some 221 pumps at intervals up the hillside, plus a complex system of hydraulics and pipework.

Even then, only the fountains close to the Palace could play continuously. When the King and his entourage, or some important visitor, toured the gardens, a highly organized routine was put into action. Boys with whistles signalled for every fountain in sight of the promenaders to be turned on and, once they had passed by, for the water to be turned off.

Water gives an extra dimension to any garden, and a fountain, however simple, the pleasure of both the sight and sound of moving water. Most gardeners with smallish plots of land are content with a single fountain, usually associated with a pool – a relatively inexpensive and easy feature to create.

The end of the vista in the painting is also worth considering as a focal point for the end of a larger formal garden, with a fountain basin, jet and statue set into a recessed, clipped hedge.

Sundials, animal figures and statuary

The Queen's Theatre from the Rotunda, Stowe. Jacques Rigaud
Private Collection.

CHAPTER THREE

LANDSCAPE

AND

FORMALITY

Gardens of the 18th and

19th centuries

THE GARDENS IN THE PARC MIRABELL, AUSTRIA

N. Diesel, c. 1720

VIENNA (HISTORICAL MUSEUM)

In the early days of European gardening, when flower cultivation was still limited, larger gardens tended to rely on using low-growing plants in patterns. The plants used were notably dwarf box and cotton lavender, which would be regularly clipped, but thyme, hyssop and similar plants were also employed. The earliest form of such patterned gardens was the knot, which can be dated to a Venetian representation in 1499.

In the 16th and 17th centuries, the knot became very much an English design feature. Mainly involving a tight pattern of planting, often resembling a tied knot, it was also made in regular designs. At first the knots would be infilled with sand, coaldust, chalk and coaldust (to make blue), broken bricks, or coloured earths, a practice which caused Francis Bacon to deride them – 'These be but toys', he wrote: 'you may see as good sights many times in tarts.' Later, the knots became more elaborate, infilled with flowering plants.

European gardeners usually made larger, more florid patterns, known as parterres. Both knot and parterre were best viewed from some height, at the level of a first-floor window. The Italians were the first to develop the parterre, an idea then taken up in France and other European countries. The French had many categories of parterre, including the *parterre de broderie* shown here – a design as if in embroidery. The pattern was almost always carried out in dwarf box, and filled, as here, with sand or some other single-coloured inert material.

The resulting permanent design, summer and winter alike, needed little maintenance apart from clipping and weeding. In this 18th century Austrian example, the parterre and wall are decorated with bay trees in tubs, while the walls on either side of the courtyard are decorated with trained and trimmed figs.

Knots are suitable for even quite small areas; the larger parterre (it is admittedly difficult to say what distinguishes a knot from a parterre), rather less so. These days both types tend to be infilled with flowers rather than with sand.

A simple knot of clipped box, with cypresses at the corners and a formally planted bed, with an ornamental standard, in the centre

THE MERCHANTS' GARDENS AT A GATE OF PARIS

Anon, 18th century

PARIS (MUSÉE CARNAVALET)

One might almost call this a puzzle picture: there is quite a lot going on if you look hard at it. The sleeping girl on the left is about to be woken by a gentleman with a flower, while the man on the centre right is carrying out some task which obviously creates a nasty smell. Near him a sheep is being shorn, a man carries a rock, and a boy in blue holds a mysterious object. On the right, the man in green seems to be carrying a surveying instrument. Within the gates, another gentleman – one can guess at his rank by his sword, and perhaps by his green parasol, is looking around, rather puzzled, with a book in his hand – a catalogue perhaps?

What exactly are these merchants selling, one wonders; is it plants, or do they just have a nice garden for their clients? It may well be plants, because the beds in the distance clearly contain seedlings or young plants in neat rows, reminiscent of a modern garden centre.

The flowers here have been depicted rather roughly. In the foreground beds, the simple wooden edgings rather reminiscent of medieval times, there appear to be tulips. The taller red flowers by the wall are peonies maybe, while the taller bushes are possibly tree peonies.

An interesting feature of this view is the way that the beds, even if they are utilitarian, are laid out in an attractive formal way, with some devoted to flowering and shrubby plants. On the walls, which are equipped with wooden trellised slats, you can just make out trained fruit trees.

In the background are square-cut hedges from which rise the straight trunks of trees which have been trimmed into large and small arches. Two blocks of these trimmed arches and attendant hedges focus the eye on a centrepiece in the distance, where the trellis is probably built using the *trompe-l'oeil* technique of false perspective to make it look as though the flat woodwork is in fact another receding arched feature.

Today, the modern equivalent of these tree arches is to be found at Hidcote, Gloucestershire, in the hornbeam stilt garden. Even these rectangularly trimmed aerial hedges on exposed trunks demand a good deal of work. To maintain trimmed arches would mean even more although it is a nice idea.

A layout of such formal beds with narrow paths between, readily created in a small garden, could be set off with a clipped hedge on a more modest scale, with perhaps a single central arch framing an ornament.

THE ORANGE-TREE GARDEN AT CHISWICK HOUSE

P. A. Rysbrack, 1729-31

LONDON (VICTORIA AND ALBERT MUSEUM)

During the 18th century one of the greatest influences on art and architecture in England was the third Earl of Burlington (1695–1753). With the aid of the famous landscape designers William Kent and Charles Bridgeman he laid out gardens at Chiswick House, London, by the Thames, based on Palladio's Villa Capra, also known as La Rotunda, near Vicenza.

It was in his *Epistle to Lord Burlington* of 1731 that Alexander Pope wrote the famous lines

> To build, to plant, whatever you intend,
> To rear the Column, or the Arch to bend,
> To swell the Terras, or to sink the Grot;
> In all, let *Nature* never be forgot.
> Consult the *Genius* of the *Place* in all . . .

It was the first time that the phrase 'the genius of the place' was used and by it, Pope implied that the designers had made good use in their plans of the natural contours and 'feel' of the site rather than wreaking massive changes upon the setting.

Within its expanse – now of course entirely surrounded by suburban housing and a busy main road on one side – there are a great many formal features, statues and classical urns, a river with rustic bridge and cascade, and several informal areas. The layout is asymmetrical, a welcome change from the regularity of its predecessors, and full of surprises as one passes through the openings off the main axis which lead to intricate walks and layouts.

This painting, one of a series of eight by Rysbrack, shows the 'Amphitheatrical Orange Tree Garden' with its domed classical temple and obelisk in a pool – a 'conceit' which Thomas Jefferson, during a tour of English gardens in 1786, noted as 'an obelisk . . . in the middle of a pond useless.' Other visitors thought better of the garden as a whole: Daniel Defoe, who described Chiswick in detail, wrote that 'the Gardens are . . . laid out in an elegant Taste . . . there is more Variety in this Garden, than can be found in any other of the same size in *England,* or perhaps in *Europe* . . .' It is certain that the garden, like its owner, had a great influence on garden design.

As explained elsewhere (see page 78) orange trees in pots were brought into shelters (not surprisingly called orangeries) to overwinter and later brought out to stand either in front of the orangery or another building. Here they are arranged in three concentric ranks as in an amphitheatre, with the water-based obelisk as the focal point. Oranges are not used for such purposes in England nowadays, but the effect could be imitated – by most of us on a very much smaller scale – with clipped bay trees trained as standards or similar evergreens kept permanently in large wooden tubs.

A PARK

Anon (English), c. 1735

LONDON (VICTORIA AND ALBERT MUSEUM)

This illustration provides an example of the grand-manner type of gardening developed by the French in the early 18th century and then taken up elsewhere in Europe. In this kind of garden, long flat vistas of canal pools gave way to huge, meticulously trimmed hedges, all focused, like most landscape vistas, on an elaborate piece of architecture. Behind the hedges groves of trees and *bosquets* (see page 48) of shrubs provided shady walks along meandering paths which usually led to other formal features.

Here trees with bare lower trunks have been cleverly placed to give height to this set-piece, and in the distance, on either side of the far pavilion, two further trees emphasize the focal point and centre the view on the distant tree-topped slope.

The courtyard, which here acts as an almost stage-like foreground, to the backdrop of the hedged perspective, is formally edged by a narrow canal with hedges on either side. Rather strangely, there is no bridge to enable one to walk directly from the courtyard to the long *allée* beyond. Patterns of formal beds, like a very open parterre, planted with shrubs and trees that one imagines will later all be trimmed into formal shapes, act as counterpoint to the blocks of green hedging beyond, and the whole is framed by elegant, very high, arcaded pavilions with arched roofs. Climbing plants are growing up their pillars, and among and behind the narrow arcade are massed, low, rounded shrubs, possibly box.

Such a layout is really only feasible where there is plenty of space in all direction, and only the best-endowed gardens could afford to retain armies of gardeners to maintain such massive hedging. This was done with the aid of wheeled platforms and scaffold-like towers on wheels, and although shears were used, much of the trimming was carried out with sickles, sometimes mounted on long handles.

One could, however, re-create the long perspective, on a more modest scale, with a pair of borders separated by a grass walk and backed by clipped hedges. To accentuate perspective where space is limited, hedges can be set so that they narrow together at the far end, and their top edges can also be trimmed slightly downwards towards the focal point.

MASON'S GARDEN, NUNEHAM, OXFORDSHIRE

Paul Sandby, c. 1760

(PRIVATE COLLECTION)

This painting, done in 1760, depicts a style of gardening that became known as 'English' rather than 'Italian' or 'French'. The estate was actually that of Lord Nuneham (later Viscount Harcourt) but it is known as Mason's Garden because the poet William Mason advised on its design. Both were admirers of the French writer and philosopher Jean-Jacques Rousseau (1712–78), who believed that nature should be altered as little as possible if it was to have the maximum effect on man's emotions, and contemporaries saw this garden also as representing that of Julie in Rousseau's book *La Nouvelle Héloise*.

Although one could hardly call this layout truly natural, its seemingly arbitrary arrangement of flower beds and shrub borders in lawn, and the arrangement of their contents, was intended to represent the natural state. In the background a Temple of Flora houses busts, including one of Rousseau, and the garden itself contains urns and inscriptions intended to accentuate the sense of, and love of, nature, together with the melancholy that these feelings were expected to evoke.

The groups of trees and shrubs are certainly informal, though their edgings of dwarf shrubs, probably box, are less so, and Rousseau might not have approved of either the Temple of Flora or of the rectangular building on the left, which seems to be a greenhouse. But this was certainly something quite different from the picturesque landscape gardens being created in parkland, also in Nature's name, at the same time. Mason's Garden, which is an enclosed one, shut off from the rest of the landscaped park, is both a landmark and a remarkably modern-seeming composition, and is presently being restored by the Garden History Society. Paul Sandby, the painter of this view, thought it 'one of the most delightful scenes that the power of imagination can form or fancy paint'.

In modern terms, what we see here are very early examples both of informal planting – very much a 20th century concept – and of the island beds which were pioneered by Alan Bloom in Britain in the 1950s. In the 'island bed', the planting, set in grass, is viewed from all sides and rises highest in the centre, whereas in a border proper the plants are graded in height from front to back, with a few deliberate irregularities. In the right place, even a smallish island bed can be most effective. Island beds, which can be of any shape desired, can easily be created wherever there is a large enough lawn, using either herbaceous perennials or shrubs, or a mixture of both.

WOODSIDE HOUSE, BERKSHIRE: THE CHINESE KIOSK

Thomas Robins the Elder, c. 1755

(PRIVATE COLLECTION)

Thomas Robins is a fascinating painter for two reasons. First, he was totally forgotten for two centuries after his death in 1770; his paintings hung, barely noticed, on the back stairs and landings of the houses concerned. Secondly, the 22 views of his we know, and his sketchbook, preserve for us a brief gardening fashion that came and went, more or less, during the years of his own career as an artist, from 1747 to 1766.

No one has written better about him than his chronicler, John Harris: 'He was a rococo artist and his gardens are the embodiment of rococo art. Through his floral frames we can view a magical remote world. Later, in France, these gardens would have been called *jardins Anglo-Chinois*. In them is displayed intricacy within a small compass, serpentine rills and paths, fret paling and "Chippendale" bridges, confections of Chinoiserie and Gothic, and whimsicalities such as root houses, rustic arbours, grottoes and hermitages.'

Virtually every one of the whimsical gardens he portrayed in his slightly primitive style have entirely vanished although fragments of them remain here and there. The orangery he painted at Woodside survives in a dilapidated state, but nothing, unfortunately, remains of the Chinese kiosk or the adjoining decorative fence. The painting is, in fact, a rare record of such a *chinoiserie* building in the 1750s.

In the foreground lawn is one of the scenes of human activity that Robins brought into so many of his paintings. Usually these were of the people from the house concerned, promenading, sitting and talking, fishing or taking tea. In this painting some of the gardeners are scything – a skilled task on a close sward – raking and sweeping the cuttings, and rolling. The lawn is bordered by a miscellany of planted trees, and on each side, and also in the close-planted grove on the left, you can see the serpentine paths so much in vogue at the time.

On the hill behind is Cooke's Hill Wood, and in front of the trees, at the highest point of a white wooden boundary fence, is the arbour seat from which Hugh Hamersley, the owner of Woodside, could look north to a panoramic view of the Thames and a corner of Windsor Forest.

A skilful carpenter could, no doubt, create a Chinese kiosk, and you can find makers of garden buildings today of similar charm. For the less well-to-do, the same spirit could be followed to choose interesting, but less expensive, statuary and garden furniture but it is possible to obtain similar, but less elaborate, ready-made garden pavilions. The painting shows that white suits a feature in such a position, and how much the pavilion is enhanced by the delicate fence on either side, rather than standing in isolation. Something similar would make an attractive feature at the end of a rectangular plot, even if there was just a wall or hedge beyond the ornamental pavilion and flanking fence.

A simple trellis work pavilion.

MY COTTAGE IN ESSEX (BEFORE AND AFTER TRANSFORMATION)

Humphry Repton, 1816
LONDON (BRITISH LIBRARY)

Landscape designer Humphry Repton, who took over the mantle of 'Capability' Brown at a time when vast landscaped estates were beginning to be broken up and gardens of just a few acres were becoming the norm, developed the then new technique of painting before-and-after views of gardens or estates he was asked to improve. He did this by painting a watercolour of the place as it actually was, and then used what he called 'slides' which were flaps of paper stuck onto the page, to show the proposed 'after' state. These were done in special red-covered sketchbooks, now known as Repton's 'Red Books', and he created one for each estate, including several of these before-and-after views with proposals for improvements.

He set out his principles in a book called *Fragments on the Theory and Practice of Landscape Design,* and the 'after' scene of his own Essex cottage garden demonstrates the principle. In the 'before' scene a low lattice fence runs between the two foreground trees, and the cottage has no more than a strip of lawn in front of it. The shops, roadway and a triangle of grass produce an open view not improved by a butcher's shop with hanging joints of meat behind the rose tripod now seen on the left.

Somehow Repton must have acquired rights on the land beyond his original plot, for in the second view he has planted a hedge along the edges of the grass triangle and taken in the pathway. Small shrubs now stand in the grass, a vine clothes the left-hand tree, and a flower bed – presumably containing some of the earliest perennial herbaceous introductions, the use of which he did much to pioneer – has been cut in the lawn. The one-legged beggar looking over the trellis fence 'before' has now been effectively banished.

It is a better-shaped, more flowery, and certainly more private scene, though as in most of Repton's designs, the result could be called a 'prettification'. By Repton's time the wide, natural-looking landscapes of 'Capability' Brown were no longer in fashion; there was less open space, more planting of trees and shrubs, often even considerable modification to the client's house.

I am not sure that this garden is itself worthy of recreation, but the lesson we can learn from it is the use of the before-and-after views, either for planning a new garden, or for replanning an existing one. Many people use a ground-plan when contemplating changes in a layout, and a refinement of this would be to use pieces of paper representing a hedge, flower-bed or pool and shifting them around till they look right. An alternative to Repton's watercolour – and few of us are so good at drawing – would be a large photographic print, over which pieces of paper representing garden features, and cut to the right scale, could be superimposed. With patience you can achieve an effect that will provide a basis for new planting.

*Gathering Flowers in a French Garden, 1888. Childe Hassam. Worcester
Art Museum, Massachusetts.*

CHAPTER FOUR

THE AGE OF

ROMANTICISM

Gardens of the 19th and early

20th centuries

IN A SHOREHAM GARDEN

Samuel Palmer, 1826-35

LONDON (VICTORIA AND ALBERT MUSEUM)

In his massive *Encyclopaedia of Gardening,* first published in 1822, John Claudius Loudon writes that 'Floriculture is obviously of limited interest and utility, compared with horticulture . . .' Accordingly he devotes great tracts of text to growing vegetables and fruit.

Plenty has been written about growing food plants from early times, and a wealth of practical information can be found in every modern gardening book. But, considering how vital the vegetable garden was for so many centuries, it is strange that there is so little evocative writing about it. Many people still grow vegetables, usually for the freshness of newly harvested produce and for the opportunity to grow unusual types and varieties as well as for the undoubted pleasure and pride of growing food by one's own toil.

One of the most evocative passages about vegetable growing comes in Virgil's *Georgics* where he writes 'I remember I saw an old Corycian who had a few acres of waste ground, not fertile for ploughing nor suitable for cattle, crops or a vineyard. However, here and there among the thorn bushes he planted his vegetables, and around them lilies, verbena, and the slender poppy, and he equalled by his devotion the wealth of kings. Returning home late at night, he loaded his table with unbought feasts.'

A relatively modern commentary by Joseph Addison in a *Spectator* article of 1712 commented that: '. . . besides the wholsome Luxury which that Place abounds with, I have always thought a Kitchin-garden a more pleasant Sight, then the finest Orangerie, or artificial Green-house. I love to see every Thing in its Perfection, and am more pleased to survey my Rows of Colworts and Cabbages, with a thousand nameless Pot-herbs, springing up in their full Fragrancy and Verdure, than to see the tender Plants of foreign Countries . . .'

Although the cost of labour has made it difficult to maintain large kitchen gardens, when Samuel Palmer painted this opulent apple tree in a Kentish kitchen garden there was no such problem. The stately progress of the lady of the house can take in the beauty of the apple blossom and the lush promise of the other produce, never mind how much poorly paid toil has gone into its creation.

In France especially, the vegetable garden – *le jardin potager* – was often a thing of beauty with dwarf box hedges enclosing the beds of produce. But even the typical four-parted British walled kitchen garden, without any prettification, could give visual pleasure in the form of impeccable rows of well-grown vegetables, and elaborately trained fruit trees on the high brick walls.

ARABELLA SPARROW

D. S. Ryder, 1848

WILLIAMSBURG (COLONIAL WILLIAMSBURG FOUNDATION)

On the back of this charming portrait of a child its sitter has attached, in later years, a label that reads: 'Portrait of Arabella "Lois" Sparrow Southworth. At three years of age – Painted by Mr David Ryder of Rochester, Mass. at my father's old home – I was sitting in the front room on a cricket [a low stool] with – strawberries in my hand to keep me quiet – at the Sparrow home on Wareham St. – 1848.'

She was mistaken about the strawberries as in her hands, and by her right foot, are raspberries, probably the native American red raspberry. As for Mr Ryder, this is the only trace he has left of his existence. In the book *American Folk Portraits* (which are in the Abby Aldrich Rockefeller Folk Art Center) there is an interesting comment on the painting: '. . . the facile handling of foliage, flowers, and landscape details contrasts sharply with the flat, wooden treatment of the child and suggests the hand of someone more accustomed to creating wall murals or other forms of ornamental painting than with portraiture.'

This comment fits in well with Mrs Southworth's note about her being painted 'in the front room'. That was clearly painted at one time, and the flowers and landscape are a later addition.

Whether we are in a corner of a real garden, overlooking the farmhouse, or in an imaginary one hardly matters, for there is no discernible layout. Some of the plants are clearly recognizable, while others are not. The pillar at the left is wreathed in Virginia Creeper (*Parthenocissus quinquefolia*), or American Ivy as it was sometimes called, which the botanical visitor Kalm noted as growing over every house and wall. The red flower at its base is almost certainly an anenome-centred dahlia: dahlias were being used increasingly in American gardens at this time and a great many different varieties were available.

To its right, the neatly grouped flowers are probably different kinds of carnation or pink, and the large orange blooms above them are undoubtedly a day-lily (*Hemerocallis*). Just to their left are some marigolds and to the right of the child is a group of old-fashioned roses with their loose, multi-petalled flowers.

The tree behind looks like a youngish specimen of the native American False Acacia or Black Locust, *Robinia pseudacacia,* with its airy, much-divided, foliage. There are more of these in the farm grounds, together with some quite young conifers, rather stylized spruces or firs that, more than likely, are the Norway spruce, *Picea abies,* which became enormously popular in the United States in the early 19th century.

By 1848 gardening was as much a part of American as of British life, and of other parts of Europe, too; nurseries and seedsmen sold home-grown varieties although many garden plants were also imported across the Atlantic. Nowhere in the United States at that time had more gardens than Manhattan and New England.

PRINCESS MATHILDE'S DINING ROOM AT COMPIÈGNE

Charles Giraud, 1854

(CHÂTEAU DE COMPIÈGNE)

Visitors ushered into the Princess Mathilde's dining-room for the first time must have been impressed by the flower- and foliage-filled surroundings of the pillared hall.

Many of the plants, like the climbing ones up the pillars and along the cornices, and the massive foliage plants against the far wall, must have been permanent although the flower display was, without doubt, a product of the estate's extensive greenhouses.

Of the foliage plants, the grape ivy, *Cissus rhombifolia,* is in evidence on both sides of the dining room, while the further pillar on the left is enveloped in a golden-leaved ivy. Some small-leaved plants at the right probably include the creeping fig, *Ficus pumila,* and a green-leaved ivy.

The bigger plants behind include some palms and a screwpine, *Pandanus veitchii,* while the bushy plants on both sides are most likely to be willow-leaved figs, *Ficus benjamina,* and the rather ragged-looking leaves at the top on the right are possibly those of a banana plant.

There are some interesting exotics among the flowering plants, although many have been too lightly indicated with the brush to be identified. However, these plants certainly include flowering anthuriums, begonias of various kinds, several bromeliads, calceolarias, cyclamen and saintpaulias. I think I can spot geraniums (*Pelargonium zonale*), and maybe an orchid or two.

In this (admittedly incomplete) list there are no foliage plants that cannot be grown today, a reminder of how widely these tropical exotics were cultivated in the mid-19th century. They were, however, eclipsed as indoor plants towards the end of the century when the incandescent gas mantle and the introduction of central heating made atmospheric conditions too difficult for them. The resurgence in interest in house plants started in the United States before the Second World War and immediately after it in Denmark and other parts of Europe.

Although we can grow, or certainly buy in bloom, all the flowering plants depicted here, the majority will be rather short-lived in a centrally heated house. They do much better in cool, damp conditions – a superb cyclamen can often be seen in a cottage window; the same plant would be dead in three weeks in the average well-heated house.

Some people maintain a moderately heated greenhouse which can easily produce flowering pot plants for the home in the winter, including calceolarias, cinerarias, cyclamen, and greenhouse-raised relations of the primrose, like *Primula obconica* and *P. malacoides.* They are easily raised from seed in early summer without any extra heat and, potted on to flowering size, will provide the colour that many people crave among the otherwise handsome and enduring foliage houseplants.

Many indoor plants can be trained over
supports, including ivies and passionflower.

THE BEY'S GARDEN

J. F. Lewis, 1865

PRESTON (HARRIS MUSEUM)

The Turks were flower arrangers centuries ago; in the 16th century, they certainly had gardeners' guilds, the members of which demonstrated both their skills and their plants in handsome arrangements during processions. Their passion for flowers and plants can be seen in tiles and tile pictures in various places, and in the fruit and flower paintings that cover the walls of the little Fruit Room in the Harem at Topkapi, Istanbul.

Although they certainly had gardens, very little is recorded about them. I wonder whether this Bey's garden is an actual scene or an imaginary one, with its super-abundance of flowers very much in English cottage-garden tradition, since the fuchsias seen here would hardly have been known in Turkish gardens at the time of the painting, but it matters little as far as the overall effect is concerned.

The demure maiden in appropriate costume is creating a flower arrangement in an elegant oriental vase, continuing a tradition as old as Roman times in Europe and older still in China. She has a mass of flowers to choose from – madonna and orange lilies, a number of roses, delphiniums, and single- and double-flowered opium poppies in many colours. She would, in fact, not have done very well with the poppies if she had not burned or boiled their stem ends before putting them into water. At best the flowers are short-lived, and to get the most from their short lives they should be picked just as the buds open. Poppies like these are better grown for their garden display, using the round blue-green seed pods, when they fatten up, in a fresh flower arrangement or in a dried-flower decoration later in the season.

The roses in this painting are mostly Tea roses – so called because their scent was reminiscent of freshly packed China tea, imported early in the 19th century when the first Tea rose also arrived in Europe. Breeding with existing varieties soon produced an extensive race of roses with long pointed buds and, unfortunately, weak flower stalks. Though some were widely grown in Britain and Europe, the Tea roses were not really hardy in these climates. However, they grow vigorously enough in their native lands, as travellers to the Near East and China can still perceive. The Hybrid Teas, popular today, are among the descendants of the Tea rose.

The big standard rose in the background, and the Canterbury bells beside it, are standing in a garden layout that we can easily imagine: it seems to be rectangular, with a path-edged lawn and a high, rose-covered wall behind. The lawn ends in terracing which continues at this side of the lawn where the girl is working.

To her right there is a lily in a pot – perhaps *Lilium longiflorum* with its strong scent – a trailing fuchsia in another container and beside it an urn holding an *Epiphyllum,* or orchid cactus, in full spectacular bloom.

Supports for climbing roses.

THE CACTUS FANCIER

Carl Spitzweg, c. 1858

(PRIVATE COLLECTION)

What a splendid character portrait this is. It embodies all the obsessiveness of someone devoted to a single type of plant – or any other major hobby for that matter. In gardening there are people devoted to all sorts of specialities – alpines, bonsai, African violets, orchids, violets, pot leeks – and there are many specialist societies devoted to these, especially in Britain. But one of the deepest-rooted specialist enthusiasms is the passion for cacti and the other succulents most people lump together under that name.

There is a popular preconception about cactophiles that they are as prickly and unapproachable as the plants they prize, but my personal experience is that they are mainly perfectly normal, pleasant, gregarious people, who do not necessarily devote themselves entirely to succulents. I have certainly known one or two who are as peculiar as their plants, but that applies in many other branches of gardening as well.

The Czech writer Karel Capek (1887–1945), in his delightful classic *The Gardener's Year*, has a chapter 'On the cultivators of cacti.' As he writes there, 'the truth, of course is that cacti deserve their special cult, if only because they are mysterious . . . You can love them without touching them indecently, or kissing them, or pressing them to your breast; they don't care for any intimacies and other such frivolities; they are hard like stone, armed to the teeth, determined not to surrender . . . A small collection of cacti looks like a camp of warlike pygmies. Chop off a head or arm from that warrior and a new man in arms will grow out of it, brandishing sword and daggers. Life is war.

'. . . But there are mysterious moments when that obstinate and surly blockhead somehow forgets himself and falls into dreams; then a flower bursts out of him . . . a sacramental flower in the midst of brandished arms. It is a great favour, and a precious event, which does not happen to everyone.'

Just such an event is being savoured here by the 'cactus-friend' of the painting. The cactus he is holding – perhaps an echinocereus – has produced seed capsules after flowering, and, as he savours his long pipe, he peers at them through his spectacles: the very embodiment of the 'quare fellow' often associated with these plants.

Among the other plants on the wall are (from left to right): a prickly pear, or opuntia; an aloe; an echinopsis; some 'orchid cacti', or hybrid epiphyllums, and an agave.

Succulents are almost all frost-tender, though they will stand quite low temperatures if kept nearly dry. But in summer they typically enjoy sun, and can be brought into the open air to harden up, when they will be more likely to produce their blooms. This is exactly what our German cactophile has done. The main garden may perhaps lie beyond the openwork arch to the right, but one suspects that it will not interest him, content as he seems with the small world of his plants, chair and reference book.

A cactus bowl

GARDENING IN THE PARK

Anon (Germany), c. 1860

LONDON (VICTORIA AND ALBERT MUSEUM)

This German scene reminds us that for every garden, large or small, there is a good deal of behind-the-scenes activity. From the 16th century to the end of the 19th, in many parks and gardens, particularly in France and to some extent in Britain, there was great twice-yearly activity when the orange and lemon trees were brought out of their conservatories to be set out in rows, usually nearby. Man-handling these huge tubs must have presented a considerable problem, which was sometimes solved with the aid of a winch.

The word conservatory seems to have been derived from the need to 'conserve' what were known as 'winter greens' – tender plants, initially mainly shrubs, including citrus trees. A huge value was placed on citrus fruits from the 16th century on, with as many as 170 varieties being recorded, and their culture stimulated the development of winter shelters which were the forerunners of glasshouses. The original conservatories, or orangeries, were high, airy buildings of brick with tall but relatively small windows in only one wall. In these, with frost kept at bay by means of simple stoves, the tubbed citrus plants stayed through the winter until the weather became mild enough in spring to put them outside, tidy them up, and doubtless feed and top-dress them.

The glasshouse shown here is a far cry from the early shelters, reminding us of the rapid advances in engineering and metallurgy which made it possible for every park, and most suburban households, to have at least one glasshouse by the mid-19th century. Cold frames, like the large one seen here, had been in use since the 17th century, mostly being used by nursery gardeners to force vegetables out of season. In the 19th century they were doubtless used more often to raise the thousands of plants needed to furnish the great summer bedding displays still seen in parks today.

An interesting aspect of the illustration here is the female gardeners working alongside the man, armed with rake, watering can and basket – something one thinks of as a modern development.

A number of plants adapt to training, including bay.

KITCHEN GARDEN AT PLANKENBERG

J. E. Schindler, 1885

REGENSBURG (STAATSGALERIE)

eauty being in the eye of the beholder, it took a painter to make a composition from this rather untidy country vegetable plot, which was, no doubt, captured by the brush exactly as it was. Presumably one is seeing the kitchen garden of a farmstead; there is no hint of any flower garden, while beyond on the right there is possibly a grass paddock beyond the fruit trees.

The staple vegetable in this September scene is the red cabbage, obviously popular in the Netherlands since several Belgian late-Impressionist and Expressionist painters depicted them as a field crop. The red cabbage was and still is used chiefly for pickling. Finely sliced, salted, and packed tightly into earthenware crocks or wooden barrels, it was allowed to ferment for a time before being covered and sealed up for winter use, like the German sauerkraut made from white cabbage.

Most of the turnips have been harvested, and there has obviously been a crop of beans. Sunflowers, the blooms which so excited Vincent van Gogh in southern France at much the same time as this picture was painted, appear here and there, their seeds beginning to ripen. These were presumably used by the farmer's wife to feed to her poultry. Young winter cabbages, to provide fresh greens in winter, occupy the middle distance, and on the left, alongside the fence, there are some rows of Savoy cabbages, very hardy and in season from autumn to spring with large tight heads.

Although there is no ornamental flower garden, flowers for cutting, presumably annuals, are certainly being grown at the far end of this area, and a few are dotted about elsewhere. The nasturtiums by the path, near the woman hoeing, were probably grown for culinary purposes: the leaves can enhance salads, and the green seeds are sometimes used like capers.

The woman is wielding a heavy, or dragging hoe, with a large metal blade at right angles to the long handle. This is an ancient tool which is still very widely used by peasants all over the world. The English writer, J. C. Loudon, writing in 1834, described how they were used in France and Spain 'as substitutes for the spade in stirring the soil of the vineyards; and they are better adapted for hilly, stony surfaces, and for men and women who do not wear shoes than spades.'

Although straight rows of vegetables, meticulously weeded, have their own artistry, I know of one attractive English garden where both vegetables and herbs have been arranged radially around circular fruit cages. Another alternative is the French-inspired *potager*, with rectangular or sometimes radiating triangular vegetable beds with narrow paths, edged with dwarf box, cotton lavender or low-growing herbs like chives – it is very pleasing to the eye, especially if decorated with ornamental cabbages, but it is harder to cultivate and achieve large crops in this decorative manner. In fact, traditional straight rows are now giving way to the moden technique of sowing vegetables in rectangles much closer together than was once thought ideal, a system that gives bigger crops of smaller produce.

*Layout for a small potager with vegetables
separated by narrow brick paths, enclosed by
a low clipped box hedge.*

WILTON HOUSE

E. Adveno Brooke, c. 1857

LONDON (ROYAL HORTICULTURAL SOCIETY)

Many people have had a hand in designing the various parts of the still-flourishing gardens at Wilton House in Wiltshire, since the first, elaborate formality was created in about 1632 by Isaac de Caus for the 4th Earl of Pembroke. One of the garden's most important features is the bridge across the River Nadder, much enlarged by the 9th Earl in the Palladian style in 1737 – it was he, known as the 'Architect Earl', who actually designed this bridge, the first of its kind in Britain.

Most of the garden today is an informal landscape of grassy sward and trees, but there are many formal features, and there is still formality, although of a different kind, in this scene of a corner by the house, depicted in 1856. The part of the garden the artist has shown was created by Lady Pembroke in the 1820s when, with the help of Richard Westmacott, she remodelled the terrace garden created by James Wyatt about 20 years earlier, altering it into the fashionable Italian style. There was a vast geometrically arranged parterre, some of which is seen here, dotted with erect Italian cypresses – the same *Cupressus sempervirens* seen in the fresco in the Empress Livia's garden room nearly 2,000 years earlier (see page 22), with much statuary and formal urns, and gravel paths instead of grass ones.

It is impossible to identify most of the plants in the parterre beds, but this was the time when tender plants from many parts of the world were avidly mass-produced in the well-heated glasshouses that were becoming popular. In the centre we can see low beds, each of only one colour, planted with low-growing plants such as echeveria, perilla, alternanthera, forms of ajuga and so on. This technique, which required close planting of immense numbers of small plants, was called carpet bedding. Nowadays geometrically shaped beds can be filled with compact flowering bedding plants with a single colour theme in each – ageratum, begonia, petunia, salvia and tagetes among those suitable.

Wirework umbrellas of conventional shape are sometimes used for training weeping standard roses. The way they have been used here suggests other possibilities – two or three clematis would be particularly suitable, and could be left permanently in position. But few modern gardeners would, I imagine, be tempted to reproduce a parterre on any scale, except in period gardens or in parks.

In the urn at right blue agapanthus, or African lilies as they are sometimes called, are blooming, and on the wire umbrella by the urn a spectacular climber has been trained. But what it is remains a mystery: the nearest equivalent in cultivation today is a mutisia, one of a number of rarely seen climbing daisy-flowered plants from Central and South America, which are now grown in greenhouses.

An alternative plan for a small parterre.

THE GARDENS OF THE GENERALIFE, GRANADA

Ludwig Hans Fischer, 1885

MUNICH (SCHACKGALERIE)

The gardens of the Generalife, outside the fortified palace of the Alhambra in Granada, are among the most famous in the world. The Generalife was made between 1314 and 1325, a little later than the Alhambra itself, as a summer residence for the princes of Granada – a fairly sobering thought when one considers the state of gardening in the rest of Europe at the time, let alone Britain or the USA. It was just one of a series of now-vanished palaces on this hillside, and its builders were the Moors who had established their first Emirate in Cordoba in 732.

Over the centuries the Spanish reconquered most of Spain, but Granada remained the last Arab state on the European continent till its final reconquest in 1492, and the 14th century saw a great burst of cultural brilliance.

The original Moorish gardens on the terraces of this beautiful sloping site have been altered and added to over the centuries, forming a remarkable link between the Moslem and the Christian civilizations. Relatively small pavilions form focal points – to a series of walled enclosures – patios in the proper sense of this much misused word. Water is used throughout, and although the arching fountain jets along this narrow canal pool are quite recent additions, they are entirely in keeping with Islamic garden tradition.

This patio seems to have had various names. It is sometimes called Patio de la Acequia from the original aqueduct, and sometimes Patio de la Riadh or Ria – it would be simpler, perhaps, to call it the 'Court of the Canal'. It is a long and quite narrow courtyard, with the canal – its level nowadays almost up to the top of the paving – interrupted in the centre by a crossway on which stands a lotus fountain bowl matching those by the pavilions at either end.

The painting shows just the end of the canal where it approaches a pavilion. At a later date this was improved by the addition of arched windows and an open, roofed terrace above the sloping roof, but sadly, the columnar cypresses which are such a feature of the painting have gone, as have the pots along the canal edges, and the planting is much more controlled than the attractive jumble of Mediterranean-climate plants seen here.

The layout of the garden is very much an Arab concept: a high-walled enclosure with a rectangular pool – usually much wider – and fountains to provide coolness and refreshing sound in a hot climate.

The concept of a narrow canal pool suits the long, narrow, town garden of today as a centrepiece for a formal layout with paving around the edges and plant borders beyond. As multiple fountain jets call for elaborate plumbing, the best and simplest alternative is a fountain jet, or a small statue embodying a fountain, placed at the further end of the pool and operated by a concealed pump. A small pavilion beyond the pool could act as a focal point.

SUNFLOWERS IN A BORDER

G. S. Elgood, c. 1890

(PRIVATE COLLECTION)

It takes a bold gardener to venture a massive and short-lived grouping like this, all of annuals and biennials. The sunflower which plays such a dominant role, is easily raised from seed but, of course, is over by late summer. The crowded lavender flowers in the foreground, some showing a distinct blotch at the base, are those of *Schizanthus pinnatus,* a half-hardy annual more often grown indoors as a pot plant than in the open garden. It is threaded by the gold, white-tipped blooms of the poached egg plant or meadow foam, *Limnanthes douglasii,* a very pleasing but short-lived annual. There is a hollyhock (another seed plant) and biennial mulleins in the distance, as well as other unidentifiable plants that have presumably all been grown from seed.

Although these temporary plants suggest the profusion of a cottage plot, they are clearly set in the border of a large garden, backed by shrubs and trees. The paved path and mossy wall alongside the steps also indicate a large and palatial setting, where expenditure on labour is doubtless disregarded.

Today gardeners rarely rely so much on short-lived plants grown from seed, except in parks and similar public places. A more practical solution for larger gardens is an 'in-between' technique where seed plants are grown among the permanent perennials and shrubs to provide plenty of summer-long colour after the spring bedders, like wallflowers and tulips, are over.

Some smaller gardens today, however, are devoted entirely to bedding plants. Hundreds, sometimes thousands, of them are raised under glass from seed or cuttings by their painstaking owners and laboriously planted out in late spring, often in the mannered patterns reminiscent of elaborate 19th century bedding schemes. The plants are chosen for brilliant colours – fiery salvias, garish gold and orange marigolds, bright blue ageratums and lobelias, but it is perfectly possible to create quieter and more sophisticated colour schemes by the use of pastel-shaded and white-flowered bedding plants like petunias, offset by silvery foliage like *Cineraria maritima* and its relatives.

You could, of course, reproduce the atmosphere of this border using less labour-intensive permanent plants. Tall yellow-flowered *Eremurus,* or a ligularia, could replace the sunflower and a lavender-blue hebe like 'Midsummer Beauty' the *Schizanthus.* Possible silvery additions are *Ballota pseudodictamnus,* cotton lavender (*Santolina chamaecyparissus*), lamb's ears (*Stachys lanata*) and the larger shrub *Senecio laxifolius,* with the bonus of golden summer flowers.

CATS PLAYING IN A GARDEN
E. B. de Satur, 1881
(PRIVATE COLLECTION)

The essence of a hot summer's day is certainly distilled here. Cats sprawl lethargically and it is too hot for the kitten to do more than pat at the rose on the grass. The heat has even caused premature dropping of the bush roses' petals.

This is basically a white garden, with the rose bushes the main feature. These are *Rosa alba maxima,* the White Rose of York, also known as Prince Charles's rose. An ancient natural hybrid in all probability, it has been cultivated since Greek and Roman times, and was a favourite subject of Italian and Dutch painters. Alongside the rose bushes, white foxgloves lift their airy spires, and to the left there is a sprawling bush of cotton lavender (*Santolina chamaecyparissus*). The plant on the brick wall behind, itself looking sun-bleached, appears to be the ornamental vine (*Vitis vinifera* 'Purpurea'), which has silvery foliage when young, taking on purplish tones as summer advances and turning deep crimson-purple before the leaves finally fall.

Below it grows what looks like a white-variegated ivy – *H. helix* 'Glacier' would be a modern example – or a euonymus like *E. radicans* 'Variegatus'. Euonymus are excellent plants for such places, some being sprawling, others more or less erect, and a few making compact shrubs. They have white- or yellow-marked leaves, and one, *Euonymus fortunei* 'Coloratus', is a rosy purple during winter.

Climbers on walls are always desirable, as they take the garden upwards, creating something from an otherwise unused vertical space. On really old walls with loose mortar ivies can cause structural problems, but in principle they are among the most valuable plants for walls and fences, even wire ones. They create a dense mass of green, gold or silver, with large or small leaves of various forms; they thrive in sun or in shade, and they give a glow of colour throughout winter – except in the coldest areas, where leaves may become damaged.

Although basically a one-colour garden, there is a little colour here, provided by a cineraria flowering in the urn on the left; a couple of pansies in the border and a sunflower blooming in the Chinese urn on the right. Gardens of one colour were popular in the late 19th and early 20th centuries, particularly in Britain, and of the colours chosen, white seems to have been the favourite. There is a classic example, still well maintained, at Vita Sackville-West's famous Sissinghurst Castle in Kent. It is worth mentioning here some of the plants she used for the benefit of anyone considering planting such a garden. There are white delphiniums (of the Pacific strain), masses of *Lilium regale,* with sweet-scented trumpets; silver-foliaged artemisias, cotton lavender, *Senecio cineraria;* white-flowered cistus, campanulas, Chinese bellflowers (*Platycodon*), tree peonies, Japanese anemones, dahlias, masses of foam-like gypsophila, two small sea buckthorns and the grey willow-leaved or weeping pear (*Pyrus salicifolia*), which overhangs a charming small stone statue by Eric Gill. A master-gardener's choice for a small, formal, walled garden.

HOTEL BELVEDERE, LOCARNO

E. A. Rowe, c. 1910

(PRIVATE COLLECTION)

Despite its southerly location, this is essentially an English garden scene, with borders in the informal style made popular by Gertrude Jekyll in Edwardian England. The only exotic touch is the paulownia tree decked in purple flowers, but even this can sometimes bloom in more northerly climes in a good season.

All the plants here are suitable for any sunny border with good soil. Peonies, both red and white, flop in luxuriant abandon towards an edging of thrift; wallflowers and a few tulips show that May is barely over, but the arrival of summer is demonstrated by the orange lily (*Lilium croceum*) – a plant of mid-level Alpine hay meadows. Delphiniums and fragrant pinks occupy high and low positions. The purplish leaves we can see on the wall must be an ornamental-leaved vine such as *Vitis vinifera* 'Purpurea'. To the right of the arch yellowish leaves are something of a puzzle, but could be another vine. On the left leaves of a loquat are splayed, a tree likely to fruit in warm latitudes.

Further Mediterranean touches come from the big earthenware urn, at present rather sparsely occupied by a trailing geranium, while the cascade of purple at right, probably also in an urn, must be purple heart (*Setcreasea purpurea*), which is now frequently used as a house plant. The alley alongside these is edged with dwarf box, whose smell in the heat is instantly evocative of hot summer days.

The arch with its handsome wrought-iron gates is echoed by a trained red rose behind, and behind that a second arch has what seems to be a white climbing rose at right. The furthest span covers another vine. These repeated archways frame a distant view of tree-covered hills beyond the garden wall, here formed into a seat. A curious piece of design is the small pool centred by a rushy plant, perhaps a yellow flag. This seems to be right in the centre of the brick arch, but is presumably just beyond it in the grassy walk.

It takes a fairly large garden to accommodate an arch like this one, but in a garden which is already walled, a cross-wall with an arch or a hedge with a narrow opening could be created making two entirely distinct areas, and providing the sense of surprise.

Although in many ways the garden portrayed here is much more English than European in feel, the big earthenware urn gives a classical touch and hints at warm Mediterranean days. The planting could easy be copied, and the southern-European flavour enhanced by using more bright bedding plants like geraniums, while a quick-growing setcreasea will provide brilliant purple colour in summer.

*Earthenware pots can be used to give a
Mediterranean feel to a garden*

THE WALLED GARDEN

W. T. Richards, 19th century

(PRIVATE COLLECTION)

Many a small garden, especially in towns, has corners exactly like this, with the enclosing walls forming an angle. Here a tree, rooted close to the wall, makes the position even less promising for plants, and it is probably shaded for most of the day. Yet there is a flourishing group here, clustering in a dry corner (the dryness is caused by both the tree's shade and its thirsty roots), showing how careful selection according to growing conditions can overcome most, if not all, problem corners in a garden.

The artist's attention to detail makes it quite easy to recognize most of these plants. They make a pleasing little grouping of distinct leaf forms, some dark and some variegated, with a few flowers to liven up the scene, some of them greenhouse plants just for the summer.

The plantain lily in the centre, *Hosta plantaginea* 'Grandiflora', is an example of a group of plants that have recently become very popular and that are by no means restricted to shady corners, nor are they the moisture-lovers some people seem to think. Botanically now known as *Hosta*, but not so long ago referred to as *Funkia*, they are grown primarily for their ribbed leaves, which can vary in shape from quite narrow, pointed ones to roughly oval with a heart-shaped base, as here (resembling those of a plantain as the name implies). There are a great number of varieties, many of them bred in Japan – native land of most hostas – and the United States. These plants are primarily grown for foliage and ground-covering; their flowers, though attractive, are only a secondary bonus.

To the right of the hosta are the round, cupped leaves of Lady's Mantle, *Alchemilla mollis,* and next to them leaves of a violet. Under the tree some bedding plants give colour in the darkest spot – a red verbena, purplish heliotrope, and a pansy.

The pink-flowered meadowsweet behind (probably *Filipendula palmata*) is an outstanding plant for part-shaded places, needing rich, moist soil to do its best, but in the background on the right a double-flowered hollyhock is looking rather less happy in the shady situation.

BORDERS AT ARLEY HALL

G. S. Elgood, 1910

LONDON (ROYAL HORTICULTURAL SOCIETY)

There are two surprising things about the herbaceous borders at Arley Hall, one being that they still look much the same as when George Elgood painted them 80 years ago, and the other that they were among the first such borders – if not *the* first – to be planted. Although many people think that herbaceous borders were the invention of William Robinson and Gertrude Jekyll in the latter half of the century, these borders were, in fact, first set out around 1846.

In the painting we can see the end of one of the long parallel borders with a tiny bit of its partner opposite. They look as though they are in a much older setting, an effect created by the long-established yew hedges with their trimmed buttresses and finials together with the elaborate arched stone 'vista-closer'. The house too looks much older than it is; in fact the whole ensemble was created in the 19th century.

It would not have been possible to create a proper herbaceous border, with a spring-to-autumn flowering season, much before the 1840s, because there were insufficient plants of the right type available. A herbaceous border calls for plants with relatively long individual flowering periods, in enough variety of colour, flower form and height to build up a series of massed, overlapping tableaux. From the days of Arley Hall, through the Robinson-Jekyll period, and between the two world wars, the border in Britain – where it ruled supreme as a garden feature – was always very long and several yards wide. It was difficult to plan, and needed considerable maintenance.

In modern times there are still a few noteworthy borders, but few gardeners can attempt such large expanses of intensive planting without help. However, small borders are frequently made, sometimes with a combination of herbaceous perennials, a range of bulbs and some shrubs.

Different types of edging for a border or bed:
from the top, terra cotta tiles with a sugar-
twist top, wrought-iron railings and bricks
stood on edge

Retreat. David Suff. Christie's Contemporary Art

CHAPTER FIVE

THE
MODERN
OUTLOOK

Gardens from the turn of the

century up until today

THE ARTIST'S GARDEN

Edouard Manet, 1881

(PRIVATE COLLECTION)

*M*anet loved flowers and greenery around him, but his gardening was not elaborate. Perhaps the most interesting thing in this delightful painting, at least from a gardening point of view, is the trelliswork structure, which rather resembles the arbours and tunnels of the early Renaissance period (see page 39) though it is more open and not clad in trained and trimmed plants to form a dark tunnel effect.

Here just a few plants, mainly the common climbing nasturtium, clamber on the open trelliswork. On the wall behind, a vine can be deduced, growing in a long narrow bed, and presumably trained upwards on wires. To walk in this arbour is clearly an experience of light and shade, a contrast of rigid woodwork and informal leaf patterns, enhanced by the white wall which reflects all the available light. The repeated arches create a loggia-like effect between upright panels on which the nasturtiums can spread their attractive circular leaves and open their trumpet-like flowers (the familiarity of this flower can blind us to its lovely and exotic patterning).

In this garden there is clearly some formality in the paths joining in an open roundel, and the shaped beds, but the planting seems almost casual. A few scarlet geraniums dot an otherwise unplanted bed in the foreground in the company of some unidentifiable green shrubs, though a bed nearer the arbour, slightly raised above the path with an edging of flints, is massed with these familiar summer plants to create a focus of colour.

Behind the bench there is another cluster of flowers which looks to be straight out of a provincial park – possibly blue cornflowers and pink mallows, though their form is barely indicated. The grass, in which are planted a couple of birches with straight white trunks and airy foliage, has not recently seen a mower – or the scythe, which Manet might perhaps have found preferable.

Though the arbour looks charming unadorned, few gardeners could resist the temptation to grow plants on it. These might be annual climbers like the nasturtiums (*Tropaeolum majus*), the related canary creeper (*T. peregrinum*) with delicate yellow flowers, or the cup-and-saucer vine (*Cobaea scandens*). For a denser effect many woody climbers are available – among them rambler roses, clematis, honeysuckle, jasmine, wisteria, passion-flower, potato vine (*Solanum crispum*), and other ornamental vines.

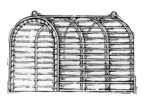

Metal tunnel arbour

BREAKFAST, SUMMERTIME

Claude Monet, c. 1873

PARIS (MUSÉE D'ORSAY)

Like his contemporary Manet (see page 98), Monet enjoyed his garden, and he and his gardeners clearly did their best to produce plenty of colour during the warm days of summer. Most that we can see here comes from the readily available, easily propagated zonal pelargonium, or geranium, which remains a top favourite today. There are both red and white varieties, and the one just in front of the woman's dress appears to have variegated leaves – one of a number of varieties now available in which leaf colour is almost as important as flower. The geraniums on the left are mounded up into a hillock topped by a variegated ivy spreading its fronds into the air – perhaps on a raised bed or by the clever use of pots grouped as a pyramid.

There is a delightful colour mixture in the border by the house. In this rather shaded spot, the red flowers are probably a bedding begonia (*B. semperflorens*). Intermingled with these are pale sky-blue flowers of love-in-a-mist (*Nigella damascena*). In front of this bed a dwarf standard fuchsia, nicely shaped, grows in a square tub, finished off with low trailing plants.

To produce dappled shade for the table in the summer heat, a vine has been trained on wires to form a rustic arbour. It must certainly have been pleasant to breakfast among these flowers and under the vine foliage, among which a lady's straw hat, decked with a white rose, has been hung to form a focal point for the composition.

Such arbours come into their own in warm countries, but are quite feasible in cooler ones, choosing perhaps the ornamental rather than fruiting vines, like *Vitis vinifera* 'Brant' and *V.v.* 'Purpurea'. In really cold places the 'Russian vine', *Polygonum baldschuanicum,* could be used instead, though it has not the same quality of leaf and is somewhat invasive.

It is interesting to see the zonal pelargonium clearly so well established at the time of this painting. The species had been introduced from South Africa in the early 18th century, in company with several others, and breeding in the 19th century created far more varieties than we have today. The French were as active in this as the British, indeed the first satisfactory white variety was 'Mme Vaucher', raised in 1860. The French were also first to produce double-flowered kinds with massive long-lasting heads, though ornamental-leaved varieties, first known as Tricolors, were the work of an English gardener.

Fuchsias arrived rather later on the scene, but again hybridists were quick to realize the potential of these fascinating flowers – apart from their intrinsic beauty, they can also be trained in various ways, such as the standard form on a single stem seen here. Huge numbers of varieties were raised in the later part of the 19th century, with the French again being active in breeding. There are now thousands of varieties of fuchsia, and an active band of enthusiasts.

Vines, whether fruiting or ornamental, are ideal for covering a pergola and providing dappled shade

THE GARDEN OF THE ASYLUM AT ARLES

Vincent van Gogh, 1889

WINTERTHUR (OSKAR REINHARDT COLLECTION)

At first this painting looks almost like arcades of buildings around a village square, but it is, in fact, the garden of the asylum to which Van Gogh went voluntarily, as an inmate, in the last two years of his life. Peaceful, bathed in Provencal sun, and bright with flowers, it is a far cry from earlier images of 'madhouses'.

Much of the planting can only be guessed at. Some of the wedge-shaped beds that form the centre of the garden are planted with pansies, and red poppies glow in the bed on the left. In the foreground, on the right, the pink and white may come from hyacinths, edged with small-flowered violas. Above them are some trimmed standard box trees, their irregular stems suggesting great age, and to their right is a dracaena masquerading as a palm.

On the far side of the quadrangle, to the left of the foreground tree, is a bed of blue irises, and to their right an oleander is in flower. But what are the brightly coloured shrubs in pots under the arches? Tea roses seem the most likely contenders, though they might just possibly be hibiscus.

The owner of the sanatorium clearly realized the therapeutic value of flowers. The layout of the central beds fits well with the formal setting, and, perhaps, echoes the need of the inmates to have something regular and ordered to contemplate.

Goldfish swim in a central round pool which reflects the brilliant blue sky, and in which – curiously off-centre – there is a little island or a fountain bowl edged with rush-like leaves.

In essence the design of the garden is a very basic form of parterre, with beds of simple shape divided by narrow paths, and with water in the central pool providing a distinct variation of texture compared with the low planting and the edging of the beds. An unsophisticated design, it is attractive and appropriate for the place and setting. As such, it could be translated readily to a modern, enclosed back garden or to a fair-sized front garden. Edgings could be of tight-clipped green box or silver cotton lavender, or dwarf bedding plants like lobelia or *Begonia semperflorens* in season. Any compact bedding plant could fill the beds, like ageratum, petunias, verbena, or pansies. Low-growing ones are essential for the design because they allow the pattern of the beds to show clearly, and permit the pool to be seen from all sides.

Bed arrangements to surround a circular or square pool, using clipped box (left) or bricks (right) as an edging.

THE WATERLILY POND

Claude Monet, 1899

In 1883, the painter Monet rented a house at Giverny in the Eure district of France. He turned the orchard into a flower garden, where rambler roses covered trellis arches and wild flowers filled the ground – poppies, annual chrysanthemums, cornflowers and corn cockles among them.

In an area of marshy ground which he acquired just outside the boundaries of the original garden Monet diverted the local river to form a large pear-shaped pool. Filled with waterlilies, fringed with weeping willows, and with a Japanese-style bridge over it, eventually surmounted by a wisteria-covered pergola, it is now famous as the subject of a series of paintings which Monet made in the latter years of his life.

In their *Dictionary of Art and Artists,* Peter and Linda Murray make the interesting point that 'it has recently been claimed that these shimmering pools of colour, almost totally devoid of form, are the true starting-point of abstract art . . . the logical outcome of Monet's lifelong devotion to the ultimate form of naturalism, truth of retinal sensation'.

The waterlily was a vital part of ancient Egyptian gardens (see page 136), and was grown by the Chinese and later the Japanese, but it was not cultivated in Europe until around 1730, when in any case there was only the wild white waterlily to cultivate, and its yellow relations.

In 1849 the first flowering of the giant South American waterlily *Victoria amazonica,* at Chatsworth in England, awoke an interest in such plants. Gardeners were clamouring for hardy kinds and in 1858 the Frenchman Joseph Latour-Marliac started to try and breed coloured hybrids, but did not begin to succeed until 1879. Having discovered how to cross these plants successfully, he then produced a spate of new hardy varieties – over 70 in all until his death in 1937 – some of which Monet obtained to create variety in his waterscape. Many of the varieties are still with us.

Although Monet chose to create a large pool, there are varieties of waterlilies for every size and type of still-water feature – from a lake to a small tub. Just as a water feature of any kind creates a new dimension in the garden, the waterlily provides a unique plant, with its handsome, waxy, multi-petalled blooms growing in the same plane as its rounded heart-shaped leaves.

Water lilies are best planted in a mesh container, filled with rich compost and topped with stones to prevent the compost being washed away

THE GARDEN AT VAUCRESSON

Edouard Vuillard, 1923–37

NEW YORK (METROPOLITAN MUSEUM OF FINE ART)

Edouard Vuillard, like his friend Pierre Bonnard, became classed as an Intimiste, using the Impressionist technique to depict ordinary domestic moments, usually indoors, rather than the customary landscapes. This painting is of a small segment of a garden, rather than an interior, but it nevertheless retains that intimate feeling, and is also reminiscent of the two-dimensional Japanese prints that so influenced Vuillard, Bonnard and some of their contemporaries.

This garden view is, indeed, curiously flat, dominated by the tangle of floriferous rose stems in the foreground, through which a haze of blue is visible – possibly a row of lavender. There are hints of other flowers along the long narrow bed, and near the post in the foreground the grey stems suggest cotton lavender (*Santolina chamaecyparissus*) with, to their right, perhaps the felted leaves of lambs' ears (*Stachys lanata*).

Behind this line of blue haze a tall hollyhock can be seen with another rose alongside it. In the background on the left the bright yellow is Scotch broom *(Cytisus scoparius)*; there are three such plants as half-standards on clear, erect stems about 3ft (1m) tall. Beyond these there are hints again of a bright border alongside the drive.

Behind the woman in pink some flowering plants are laid out in neat rows; they look like bedding geraniums, but they could also be flowers for cutting. The bed is edged with a green plant fronting a path, probably dwarf box, while to the left of the picture the green edging expands to include some bright red and pink flowering plants to form a border to a lawn.

The great English gardener, William Robinson, recorded, in Paris in 1867, that the borders there contained not only the tender annuals popular at the time, but also 'permanent things – lilac bushes, roses, etc. which give a line of verdure throughout the centre of the border, and prevent it being quite overdone with flowers'. The long, narrow border in Vuillard's painting is quite modest and seems to be relatively low between the rose bushes, dividing the gravel walk at right from the lawn.

Although there is nothing elaborate about this garden it is obviously a pleasant place, particularly on a warm summer's day when the flowers vibrate with colour. The woman in the picture is probably Lucie Hessel, Vuillard's neighbour at Vaucresson and the wife of the art dealer Joseph Hessel, who had acquired the house and garden in exchange for a painting by Cézanne.

FARM GARDEN WITH SUNFLOWERS

Gustav Klimt, 1905-6

VIENNA (ÖSTERREICHISCHE MUSEUM)

*H*ere is a veritable tapestry of flowers. A curious mixture, mostly of low-growing plants, it is dominated by the huge sunflower – an annual which can easily exceed 3.1m (10ft) tall, with a white, pink-eyed perennial phlox in the foreground playing a supporting role. The orange blooms to the left of the sunflower are almost certainly a single-flowered dahlia, but the rest of the plants all appear to be annuals.

Eleanor Perenyi wrote of annuals in *Green Thoughts* that although they set seed and die within a single season '. . . they can perform prodigies in their brief lives. A morning glory will throw a blue mantle over a small building in no time, tithoniums and castor plants make hedges tall as a man by midsummer.'

In Klimt's painting every flower, except the phlox, is round, and almost every one seems to be a composite or daisy relation. Golden marigolds, cornflowers and annual asters provide the blue and lavender shades, and there are pink double daisies and annual chrysanthemums and, probably, some everlasting flowers like helichrysum (or straw flower), all covering every inch of soil.

There is no apparent garden form: the painting simply shows a patch of ground where annuals have been sown in mid-spring for a profuse summer display. One can imagine the farmer's wife creating such a display near her kitchen window, perhaps, to give her this heart-warming profusion of colour to look out on during the summer.

Although this sounds easy, it only works properly on light, easily worked soil, as it is often difficult to get the seeds to germinate in heavier soils. The soil is forked over and raked to a fine tilth, the seeds are then scattered over it sparingly, so that they do not germinate too close together, and then are raked over so that they are just covered. As the seedlings appear they need thinning out to prevent them becoming congested.

There are many wonderful annuals apart from the common ones, which good seed catalogues display in tantalizing photographs. There is no need to limit yourself to the well-known petunias, salvias, French and African marigolds and the like, sold in millions by the garden centres for planting out as seedlings. Annuals come in every height and colour, to provide a Joseph's coat of blooms, as Klimt's painting shows, including climbers and creepers. All they ask for is lightish soil, plenty of sun, proper thinning out and, if possible, dead-heading to perform till the first frosts come.

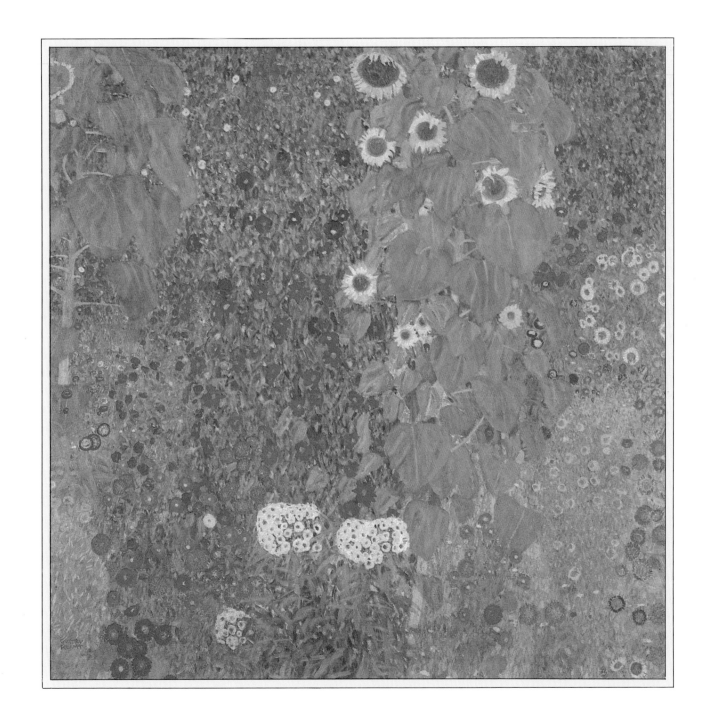

THE DREAM

Henri ('le Douanier') Rousseau, 1910

NEW YORK (METROPOLITAN MUSEUM OF FINE ART)

Henri Rousseau (known as 'Le Douanier', because he worked for the Paris municipal customs service) was probably the most famous 'Sunday' painter of all times. He painted several elaborate and exotic jungle scenes, of which this, his last work, is one. It was disparaged by one critic as being impossibly naive in portraying a woman on a couch in the midst of a jungle, but Rousseau had a perfectly reasonable reply. 'The woman asleep on the couch is dreaming that she has been transported to this forest and that she can hear the enchanter's music. That is the explanation of the couch in the picture . . .'

Many of Rousseau's jungle plants, like his animals, are more or less recognizable; he must have had botanical books to use as reference for his paintings. Among the plants in this painting are the Indian lotus flowers, those emblems sacred to Buddha, with their splendid long-stemmed, multi-petalled flowers above huge waxy, circular leaves. These normally, of course, emerge from the still waters of a lake or formal pool.

At the bottom right there is undoubtedly a 'mother-in-law's tongue' (*Sansevieria trifasciata* 'Laurentii'); perhaps the yellow sword-like leaves on the left are a related plant. The other foliage is less easy to define, but some shapes are reminiscent of those familiar houseplants, dracaenas and cordylines, and the bird in the centre is sitting on a palm bough, though the orange-like fruits are incongruous.

None of this matters much; it is the dream that counts, with its music-making enchanter, the inquisitive lions accompanying him, and the birds and monkeys in the trees. One can imagine the warmth and humid atmosphere and the incessant noise of a jungle, from birds and especially insects; though perhaps here they would be stilled by the sound of the enchanter's pipe.

One could not recreate this dream-like setting in a temperate garden, because the quality of these tropical plants is quite distinct from hardy ones; but something of this atmosphere can often be found in exotic tropical gardens, or even in good-sized greenhouses, where the plants have been grouped closely together as they are in a real jungle.

With the right choice of plants even a conservatory in a temperate climate can achieve a similarly luxuriant effect, providing a strong contrast to cold winter weather outside. The Indian lotus can be grown in a tank of warm weather, and foliage plants in large attractive earthenware pots. Massed foliage is the keynote, though most of us will be satisfied to sit more conventionally clad than Rousseau's dream-transported lady.

Some suitable plants for quite cool conditions (minimum about 47°F (8°C) includes large ferns like *Woodwardia radicans,* Norfolk Island pine (*Araucaria excelsa*), bottle-brush (*Callistemon*), Chinese bamboo (*Nandina domestica*) and true bamboos, Swiss cheese plant (*Monstera deliciosa*), bird-of-paradise flower (*Strelitzia reginae*), house lime (*Sparmannia africana*), *Yucca elephantipes,* with climbers such as *Jasminum polyanthum, Lapageria rosea* and Cape leadwort (*Plumbago capensis*).

Palms and a Boat Lily (right) make a handsome group of plants for a conservatory

COTTAGES AT BURGHCLERE

Stanley Spencer, c. 1929

CAMBRIDGE (FITZWILLIAM MUSEUM)

As Anne Scott-James has written, 'the cottage garden of our dreams, with its mixture of flowers and neat rows of nourishing vegetables, is largely a Regency and Victorian conception.' Today the phrase evokes a garden informally planted, without much pattern except perhaps division into two halves by the garden path, with all sorts of perennial and annual plants in the proverbial 'riot of colour', quite often mingled with vegetables.

Until the end of the 18th century, vegetables, herbs and livestock were certainly the main ingredients of the cottager's garden, with perhaps a few flowers for decoration. As times changed, so did the cottagers' needs and aspirations; flower seeds were easier to obtain, and of course as the 'dream' cottage garden took shape people would give away and exchange choicer plants till many a tiny plot held rare treasures. Some still do, as people rediscover in such places long-lost varieties of pansies, say, or pinks.

Nowadays many cottages are owned by town dwellers as second homes and the traditional cottage garden has largely disappeared. The weekender tends to keep his plot as simple and maintenance-free as he can, since his gardening time is so limited.

These pre-war Burghclere cottages are no longer humble homes but their gardens are certainly casual. The one on the left displays the typical basis of a garden divided into two halves, and a jumbled mixture of flowers which include the perennial white Shasta daisy (*Chrysanthemum maximum*), achillea, calendula, delphiniums as well as some unidentifiable purple blooms. The cottage at the right has its flowers much more neatly planted, but unidentifiable, behind two clipped evergreens of disparate size.

For real idiosyncrasy, however, there are the two geometrical topiary shapes on the right. Almost certainly of yew, they are obviously old and have deteriorated a little; it is very difficult to keep elaborate topiary in perfect condition without regular and very expert attention. Although you can see some remarkable representational topiary today, the English tradition is for the geometrical, and many a village boasts a fanciful leafy monument of this kind, painstakingly trimmed by successive owners.

The hedges consist of a variety of plants, especially the one in the left centre which has, rather unusually, been clipped. Between the outer hedges and the road there is some wild growth which includes hazel and brambles. The path from the open gate leads between lower borders the left-hand of which holds the grassy foliage of massed daffodils.

In some ways, this painting epitomizes the saying that 'an Englishman's home is his castle'; the massive hedges, although low, effectively shut each owner's creation firmly in. The consistent white picket fences, however, reflect a typical village's cohesion.

A selection of simple topiary forms

FLOWER GARDEN, BERMUDA

Winslow Homer, 1899

NEW YORK (METROPOLITAN MUSEUM OF FINE ART)

There is a striking immediacy about this watercolour which can be traced to the artist's Civil War experience, when as an illustrator for *Harper's Weekly* he worked beside early photographers. Their photographs gave him ideas about creating three-dimensional effects on the flat canvas, though his quasi-Impressionism (as it has been described) was equally derived from pre-Civil War American painting.

There is nothing complicated about this sub-tropical garden – what there is of it reflects the low-key, away-from-it-all, holiday feeling of this tranquil scene. A border of bright colour overlooks an expanse of blue-grey which looks like water at first sight, but as there are chickens on it must be earth or sand, with a few wispy plants in it. The huge leaves are those of banana plants; to the left is a palm, and near the bungalow, by the running child, is a low leafy plant, perhaps an anthurium.

The flowers are cannas, sometimes called Indian Shot after one particular species, *Canna indica,* that has black, shot-like seeds. Nowadays, and indeed when this picture was painted, garden cannas are highly mixed hybrids derived from perhaps as many as a dozen species, all of which are of New World origin. They offer both size and brilliance of bloom with large leaves that look a bit like scaled-down banana foliage and which, in some strains, is a striking brownish purple.

Cannas are usually grown from pieces of the thick, fleshy roots or rhizomes. In warm climates they continue in leaf all year round, but in temperate zones they die down in autumn, and the roots have to be dried off and protected from frost. In spring, pieces of rhizome with a bud are started into growth in the warmth before being planted outside once any danger of frost has passed.

In northerly climes they certainly bring a tropical touch to any garden. In their native habitat they are very much in keeping with all the other exotics that have now become world-wide garden plants for those zones – the bougainvilleas, frangipanis, caesalpinias, allamandas, hibiscuses and so many more which, like the cannas, are easily grown.

In a holiday home no more is needed from a garden. The plants virtually look after themselves with little need for attention – lush greenery for restfulness and shade, brilliant flowers to echo the sun, around an open patch which can be used for games. A seaside holiday home in a temperate climate could capture the spirit of this garden with gaily painted furniture and some tough, colourful shrubs.

Coconut palms, banana plants and yuccas (from left to right) make ideal subjects for poolside containers, providing an exotic atmosphere

MA MAISON

Henri Martin, c. 1920

(PRIVATE COLLECTION)

French artists of this particular era seem to have had a special liking for zonal pelargoniums, or geraniums; but possibly this may be just a reflection of the average Frenchman's disinclination to bother with herbaceous borders and shrubs. Instead plants and cuttings of these easy plants are overwintered, guaranteeing a bright display the following summer. Most of the permanent planting here, in the bed beyond the pool, appears to be ground-cover, possibly ivy.

Besides the geraniums, which are the main providers of colour, a red and purple fuchsia overhangs the water in the foreground, and a pot of a very double fuchsia in purplish shades stands on the low wall on the right. The blob of orange across the pool, which some might find unharmonious, must be an African marigold (descendant of *Tagetes erecta*), in contrast to the smaller French marigold (*T. patula*). Tagetes are strictly annuals to be raised from seed each year, but they go on flowering until the onset of autumn frosts.

The red foliage on the outhouse to the right is clearly a Virginia creeper, probably *Parthenocissus quinquefolia*. This implies an early autumn scene, confirmed by the two shrubs in the elongated terracotta pots, which are *Hibiscus syriacus*, sometimes called tree hollyhock. At the time of this painting this blue-violet variety was probably 'Coelestis', though today 'Blue Bird' is a better one to choose for a shady site like this, and there are many different varieties in other colours. To their right low plants grow in a bed by the house wall, the pink being verbena.

The bold brushwork makes it very difficult to identify the other plants that inspired the painter. The blue that carries on along the house wall may simply be a colourful patch of shadow, but might be the shrubby frost-tender climber *Plumbago capensis,* or possibly morning glory, usually labelled *Ipomaea rubro-caerulea,* but more correctly *I. tricolor.* The best variety of this annual climber is the aptly named 'Heavenly Blue', and it is quite easily raised from seed. Given thin support to twine up, its transient blooms are produced in long succession.

To the right, in front of the Virginia creeper, there is a lot of colour discernible in the thickly applied paint. In the white container, this might be a group of cannas, with their purplish stems.

This would be quite an easy layout to create, with either potted plants or beds of annuals. The three-quarter circle of the pool with its low edging is backed by a wall into which, judging by the agitated brushwork in the water area, a fountain is splashing below the white statue. Although the perspective is a little odd, one imagines that the pool faces the entrance to the house and the path leading from it, while the green-filled beds sweep around it on either side. In a small rectangular garden you could position such a design symmetrically at its farther end, with perhaps a stretch of grass around it and with beds on either side.

A lion's head fountain and a small semi-circular raised pool

MADONNA LILIES

E. Chadwick, c. 1925

(PRIVATE COLLECTION)

The Madonna lily (*Lilium candidum*), dominates these borders. This fragrant flower, native of the Balkans, is certainly one of the oldest in cultivation, known to the Assyrians and the Minoans of ancient Crete. It was grown, and widely spread, by the Romans, and became an important herbal plant as well as being the emblem of the Virgin Mary.

Here this much-loved plant is used in cottage-garden style in wide borders stretching away from what is clearly the back of a large house – probably just one among a number of garden features. A medley of plants including the orange lily (*L. croceum*), lychnis and delphiniums, campanula, pinks, Canterbury bells, nasturtiums and a plantain lily, or hosta, is jumbled together, spreading over the stone-edged gravel path.

Part of the charm of such borders is the way that plants such as the white lychnis, foxgloves and nasturtiums will seed themselves, popping up in unplanned spots, but easily removable if really out of place. Almost all the plants here are permanent, though the Canterbury bells will have been planted in any empty gaps.

This is not a style for the purist who wants to build up carefully orchestrated associations of colour, but it can be remarkably successful in gardens large or small. It is not as labour-saving as it may seem, though, since surplus seedlings and weeds have to be dealt with early in the season and some tactful staking and tying will be needed – those lilies would not stand a storm. There will also be deadheading and cutting back of plants as they finish flowering, and later in the season the gaps may need careful filling in. But it could well be worth the effort; the happy abandon of the plants jostling together has great charm.

Plants in these borders include the following (in each case from above downwards): Left border: Delphiniums, Madonna lilies (Lilium candidum); foxglove; Shirley poppy; Lilium croceum; Canterbury bells; Lychnis coronaria 'Alba'; nasturtiums. Right border: Delphiniums; Madonna lilies; Canterbury bells; pansies; 'Mrs. Sinkins' pink; Campanula persicifolia 'Alba'; a hosta; iris (foliage); Centaurea cineraria.

GREENHOUSE PLEASURES

D. S. Vogel, c. 1937

DALLAS (VALLEY HOUSE GALLERY)

In his poem *The Task*, published in 1785, William Cowper wrote

'Who loves a garden loves a greenhouse too.
Unconscious of a less propitious clime,
There blooms exotic beauty, warm and snug.'

If there was 'exotic beauty' in 1785, how much more is there today when plant hunters have amassed specimens from most parts of the world, and breeders have developed them in various ways!

This picture shows quite a large structure, probably a conservatory, for it seems to have an arching roof and is clearly designed for displaying plants that are in flowering perfection, rather than for growing them to that stage. A bench in the foreground is full of carefully chosen colours, with plenty of white to mute the orange on the left and the red in the centre.

The impressionist rendering makes it impossible to be sure what these plants are, but the red may be a geranium and the white and yellow are probably begonias of the 'Multiflora' tuberous kind, which have a wide colour range. Some of the blue flowers are likely to be *Campanula isophylla* or *C. fragilis,* both of which make fine pot plants, and some may be 'mophead' hydrangeas, grown to produce one large flowerhead on a short stalk. The orange at right seems a little out of keeping with the colour scheme: it is possibly a lily, such as *Lilium hollandicum.*

There are more campanulas and begonia-like plants on the staging behind the people, with some ivies among them to trail over the edge and mask the hard line.

There seem to be more begonias in the colourful hanging baskets; probably the 'Pendula' forms, again tuberous, the hanging stems of which bear single or double blooms. The red and yellow flowers of these are mingled with blue ones, probably campanulas again, and the large basket at the left includes some pink, perhaps busy lizzie *(Impatiens).*

The large plant in a hanging basket at the right has the spraying habit of an *Aeschynanthus,* a tropical relation of *Gloxinia* which in full flower is spectacular indeed with clusters of erect, tubular, red blooms. Under the big basket, the yellow and red colours are characteristic of the flower clusters of the 'marmalade bush' (*Streptosolen jamesonii*) often grown as a standard on an erect stem.

With its humidity and odour of damp earth, and perhaps of fragrant flowers in the still atmosphere, a conservatory is always a different world to the outside garden. Most of all, of course, it scores in winter, when it can be kept warm and, as here, full of colour – a welcome sight compared with the chill and usually dreary aspect of the garden outside. Even a small conservatory can provide a very colourful welcome; with thermostatically controlled electric heaters, and temperatures around 45°F (7°C) plants like cinerarias, primulas and cyclamens can make a permanent display.

A glazed Victorian-style window box makes an ideal mini-conservatory where space is limited.

THE GREENHOUSE

Eric Ravilious, 1935

LONDON (TATE GALLERY)

The artist probably found this scene in one of the vast growing houses – as opposed to conservatories – that many grand houses retained right up to the Second World War – amazing as it may seem today. The scene certainly evokes days when labour was plentiful and cheap.

Greenhouses began to be fashionable even for quite ordinary people in the early part of the 19th century, when the old-style orangery (see page 57) gave way to span-roof houses with glass on roof and sides. Growing houses such as this one would fulfil the desire to have a conservatory well stocked with flowers at every season, and endless fruit and vegetable supplies for the kitchen. The glasshouses were looked after by many gardeners, ranging from the awe-inspiring head gardener and his immediate deputies to lower ranks and garden boys, lowliest of all, who lived in a 'bothy', a house of varying facilities in which they slept, ate and took whatever leisure they were allowed when not slaving in the garden.

This particular glasshouse is an example of mass-production. Up the roof members tomatoes are trained, plant upon plant, tied meticulously to wires as they extended, and carefully de-shooted so that each was a single stem. It is interesting that these are clearly a yellow-fruited variety, indicating a gourmet's choice, for the yellow-fruited kinds – first introduced by British growers in 1852 – are particularly sweet and well-flavoured, although not the most prolific croppers. Yellow varieties were known to the tropical American farmers who gradually developed the tomato from its small-fruited ancestors from western South America, but it was the red varieties, originally known as 'love apples' (they were believed to be aphrodisiacs), and also grown for decoration, that caught the public fancy in Europe.

The cyclamen growing below the tomatoes is an old-world plant, the modern strains of which were derived from *Cyclamen persicum* from the Eastern Mediterranean. This is a sweetly scented plant with delicate, airy flowers, in many shades of pink and red as well as white. Probably brought into Europe by the Crusaders, it was grown as a speciality plant in greenhouses, for it is not frost-hardy. It became a commercial pot-plant early in the 19th century, with growers constantly selecting for bigger flowers. It is always grown from seed commercially, since the tubers are relatively difficult to keep. Around 1870 a curious genetic leap occurred in both Germany and Great Britain, when plants being grown in the usual way suddenly developed very much larger flowers, in what is called gigantism. This caused much of the scent of the wild original to be lost, but it has been recovered in some modern strains, both the large-flowered ones and others which recapture the original grace of the species. In many modern strains the leaves are heavily marked with silver, or are almost entirely silver, as the artist has portrayed them here.

To grow cyclamen properly is quite a long process. Seed is sown in August and the resulting plants grown on till they are in 5 or 6 in (12.5 or 15 cm) pots, when they should flower in November of the following year. In reasonably cool conditions a cyclamen plant will flower for many winter weeks, but our living rooms are mostly too hot for their liking, and they often die after two or three weeks.

Cyclamen persicum

VICTORIAN MEMORY

Sue Wall, 1982

NEW YORK (ARTIST'S COLLECTION)

This is one of a series of fantasy paintings in which the artist has depicted houses and plantings. Victorian style is intricately rendered to the smallest details of tiling and fretwork in the imaginary mansion, which seems to be untenanted, with blinds down in all the windows. Curiously, though, the window boxes are watered and the creeper under control but no one seems to have taken much care of the grass in the foreground, behind which what appear to be hydrangeas are in flower.

In the window boxes the most readily imagined flower is the 'geranium' or zonal pelargonium, which certainly puts up with minimal watering all summer long till frost comes. There are very many homes where window boxes are the only place for any gardening and, given maximum attention, beautiful displays can be maintained. Seasonal displays are necessary in temperate climates, perhaps one for the summer and one for winter and spring. In summer there is a host of bedding plants to be selected from, which can be mingled with tuberous-rooted begonias, perhaps. You can easily be tempted to plant too early but do remember that a hard frost can destroy tender plants.

For winter the choice is more limited. Colour can be created with winter-flowering pansies, which bloom in any mild spells; or a long-term effect can be obtained with wallflowers, which have a long blooming period from spring onwards, and can be mingled with dwarf bulbs including the lower-growing tulips. A display entirely of bulbs will look empty till they start pushing up in late winter, unless combined with some evergreens such as hebes or conifers.

Where window boxes are the only gardening outlet, replanting whenever the display ends or falters is certainly worthwhile. Regular and quite copious watering is essential, for the soil in a box dries out surprisingly quickly, especially in windy places. Frequent feeding with a liquid fertilizer is also needed for the small volume of soil has to sustain the plants for months on end.

The climbing plant that is performing so well in this painting is an artist's hybrid, owing something, perhaps, to a climbing rose and something to an abutilon or hibiscus in its flower and leaf form. Flowering climbers help to soften and brighten a house front. Although there are a few self-clinging ones, like Virginia creepers and the climbing hydrangea (*Hydrangea petiolaris*), most need tying in to a support. This can be in the form of wires or a trellis, depending on the size and habit of plant concerned. Climbers do need some attention, to keep them from hiding windows, blocking gutters or getting under tiles, and they also need regular tying in as they grow. Large-flowering climbing roses or clematis on a neat trellis are among those more easily grown and controlled.

A winter window box arranged with, from left to right, florist's chrysanthemum, ivy and Christmas cherries

THE FLOWER ARRANGER

Anthony Green, 1982

LONDON (ROWAN GALLERY)

This is a self-portrait, and an autobiographical one too, one of some 25 paintings of the artist's Cambridgeshire garden. Flowers have been an important part of Anthony Green's life from his early childhood, and his garden is vital to him.

It is the late afternoon of a sunny day in early summer. The focus of the painting, of course, is the generously filled vase of flowers – honeysuckles, perennial cornflower (*Centaurea montana*), the hardy *Geranium ibericum* and cow parsley. These flowers have had much of what the artist calls 'offending foliage' removed. Beside the vase a glass holds daisies, clover and a small cow parsley head; the daisies are culled from the lawn, which the artist is reluctant to cut.

An enclosed garden, it is little larger than a room, with the house in one corner and a vegetable plot on the right, its prolific produce in the neatest of rows. The planting is not spectacular, rather the opposite; among the shrubs and lesser plants below them a pink rose to the right and the honeysuckle all over a shed in the background are the brightest flowers. Between the two there is a single-flowered white climbing rose, perhaps 'Kiftsgate'.

White flowers below the rose are, by the artist's own admission, ground elder (I hope he has not lived to regret allowing this indestructible weed to grow!) To the right the blue, next to a foxglove, is *Brunnera macrophylla*, the leaves of which are eaten with relish by the artist's fox terrier, whenever he gets the chance.

There is promise of further interest in the climbers on the house walls, while the principle of achieving a little surprise even in a tiny plot is achieved by its odd shape, making the corner to the right of the picture invisible from much of the house.

Every garden should be able to provide cut flowers for enjoyment like this. If the gardener is loth to spoil the components of the actual garden design, flowers for cutting can be grown in a separate plot, tucked away in a corner or at the end of the 'suburban strip'. Easier than growing vegetables in many cases, it probabiy achieves a good deal more saving in monetary terms.

In a plot of around 10 by 25 ft (3 by 8 m) you could grow ten useful rows of seasonal cutting flowers, which might include daffodils, tulips, pyrethrums, other summer perennials like achilleas and shasta daisies (*Chrysanthemum maximum*), sweet peas on supports, gladioli, dahlias and hardy spray chrysanthemums.

PARADISE COURTYARD

David Suff, 1982

LONDON (CHRISTIE'S CONTEMPORARY ART)

An attractively patterned grille protects the archway and the contents of this tiny courtyard from passers-by, but allows a look at the plants illuminated by overhead sunlight. One imagines a Mediterranean setting; certainly the grille, the arch and the big earthenware pot combine to give this feeling, but otherwise it could be anywhere. The plants are what those living in temperate climes call house-plants, needing to be brought indoors before winter frost but enjoying fresh air and rain during the summer.

No particular arrangement has been made of the pots and baskets, except that they have been placed at a distance from the door of the house, giving the occupant easy access to his pocket jungle. There are hanging baskets near the outer arch, and plants in containers are fixed to the back wall to provide more interest on the white surface.

At least some of the plants are identifiable. Near the centre stands an India-rubber plant (*Ficus elastica*), and to its right the much-divided leaves are those of a Norfolk Island Pine (*Araucaria imbricata*), always an elegant plant, with its branches appearing in equal-spaced tiers which in time droop from the horizontal. There is a trumpet lily in a pot, and a tropical flowering plant, an achimenes, puts out reddish flowers from a pot fastened to the wall. This is sometimes called the 'hot-water plant' because tradition holds that it is best watered from a hot kettle; if the water is not quite boiling, the steam in a pot-saucer would certainly help provide suitable humidity around it. Just below, to the right, another wall-pot seems to contain the 'purple heart' (*Setcreasea purpurea*), whose leaves provide the strongest purple leaves in the houseplant palette.

Behind the arch, at the top, there are two spider plants (*Chlorophytum comosum*) in hanging baskets, their long leaves drooping. A cascade of plantlets – the 'spiders' of the name – descend on the long flower-stems, ready to be plucked off and rooted individually when more are wanted. At top left, heart-shaped leaves suggest the 'sweetheart vine' (*Philodendron scandens*), also in a basket or high pot – one of the easiest climbers-cum-trailing houseplants.

A hanging basket planted with various ferns

FRUITS OF THE SPIRIT

Martin Charlot, 1983

(THE ARTIST'S COLLECTION)

This is a huge painting 10 by 13 ft (3.1 by 4 m) very like several murals created by Martin Charlot for various instiutions in his native Hawaii. Mural painting was in his blood, for his father, Jean Charlot, taught the art of the fresco to Diego Rivera and many other Mexican painters in the 1920s and '30s.

The inspiration of *Fruits of the Spirit* came, apparently, from watching the children of Waiahole Valley jump into a pond. The artist, who took his title from Psalm 127: 'Lo, children are a heritage of the Lord and the fruit of the womb is His reward,' has written of the scene that, 'They seemed to be flying, and in flight they embodied all the joy and unfettered freedom of childhood and the spirituality of innocence uncorrupted.' To obtain images of children 'flying' he took a trampoline to the local school and photographed the children – including some of his own – in various aerial poses. The child in the centre foreground is the 'hip' kid who cannot understand how other children can possibly fly.

It is a picture symbolizing fertility and plenty in a lush Hawaiian valley with a waterfall and rocky stream. Here flowers and fruits show the potential abundance of the tropics and the abandon in which they can grow. In some measure you could regard the scene as another version of the Garden of Eden, such a powerful inspiration for the earliest Middle Eastern gardens; the whole idea of the garden as paradise began there and continues (if largely subconsciously) to influence garden makers today (see pages 18-19). The Garden of Eden was depicted many times in painting, of course, in various versions of the idyllic landscape in which Adam and Eve meet their fate, and mankind's, from the serpent.

There is no serpent, though, in this happy scene of natural abundance, with breadfruit, stilt-rooted screwpine, fruits and flowers of many kinds.

Although the plants seem haphazardly arranged, the area in the foreground to the right of the stream could pass for a bit of deliberate planting, with the mass of low, flowering plants – *Impatiens* perhaps, edged with some bolder foliage plants. In the background trees are draped with climbing plants as so often happens in the tropics, something gardeners in cooler climates can achieve by growing climbers, like strong climbing roses or clematis, into the crowns of old fruit trees for instance.

The plants and fruits in this painting include: pink passionflower (top left); coconut (sprouting); pawpaw (opened-up fruit); heliconia (upper right); breadfruit (top right); dracaenias; screwpine (plant with stilt roots, fruit in right foreground); Bird-of-paradise (Strelitzia reginae, right centre); mangoes; pineapple; ginger lily (Hedychium coronarium, lower right); apé (Xanthosma rosea); (large leaves); Hibiscus rosa-sinensis; various palms.

THE GARDEN PATH

Louis Turpin, 1986

(PRIVATE COLLECTION)

We can hardly play the identification game with this modern vision of a herbaceous border. True, in the centre there are undeniable yellow and orange daisy flowers, probably rudbeckias, but the other flowers are reduced to splashes of colour. The red on the right looks poppy-like and is perhaps the double scarlet selection of Shirley poppy called 'Dazzler'. The liking for ornamental grasses, with their spraying foliage, is a modern trend – they are very useful for providing a contrast to bright flowers as well as a permanent backdrop for the different perennials as their flowers come and go. The white upright grass is probably 'gardener's garters' (*Phalaris arundinacea* 'Picta'), or the similar and less invasive *Miscanthus sinensis* 'Variegatus'.

The brilliant scene is backed by great massifs of a yew hedge, with the entrance – the path of the title – leading to some mysterious enclosed grass walk. And behind this formality, what are the trees? Their tiered regularity suggests that curious Australian relative of the monkey puzzle, *Araucaria bidwillii,* so often seen in Mediterranean lands and the southern United States. But in an English garden, as this surely is, they must be conifers: perhaps Scots pines which the artist has reshaped.

In one way, this painting is just reflecting a modern impressionistic technique: it does not really matter what the plants are. And one may also ask oneself if this is not the best way of looking at a herbaceous border, or indeed any other plant association where a good blend of colours and textures is important. There is a modern obsession with the individual plant which makes most garden viewers walk along with either a real or mental notebook, trying to identify each component.

A few painters have been good gardeners, and the greatest as a gardener was certainly Gertrude Jekyll (1843–1932). Born in the heyday of Victorian bedding schemes, she and her contemporary William Robinson became the two most influential advocates of a switch to naturalistic planting. They did not actually invent the herbaceous border, but they virtually ensured that it would hold sway until, after the Second World War, it became too labour-intensive to be an everyday feature.

I am not sure that Gertrude Jekyll would have approved of the border Louis Turpin has portrayed, with its strong colour juxtapositions; but her main principles have been followed: start with colours and then work out planting.

An Old Garden, Ella du Cane (from The Flowers and Gardens of Japan *by
Florence du Cane (A &C Black)*

CHAPTER SIX

THE
ORIENTAL
LEGACY

The gardens of Asia and the

Middle East throughout the ages

THE GARDEN OF NEBAMUN

Egypt, c. 1400 BC

LONDON (BRITISH MUSEUM)

Among the paintings of ancient Egyptian gardens found on the walls of tombs is this remnant showing the garden of Nebamun, 'a scribe who keeps account of the corn of Amun'. It is probably not an actual garden but a representation of a symbolic one, where the person to whom it is dedicated could refresh himself in the afterlife. This explanation is reinforced by the figure of the woman at top right, who is arranging the offerings which a recently buried person would receive from his family.

Gardens in ancient Egypt were always formal and usually symmetrical, as in this small plot, their basic principle being of a rectangular pool surrounded by trees. The largest gardens might surround the house, or at least have several pavilions in which to sit, muse and enjoy the scene.

The Egyptians had few native plants, and their gardens concentrated on fruit-bearing trees, which also provided greenery and shade in a hot, dry and unwooded country. Their pools, however, would hold the native white waterlily or Egyptian lotus (*Nymphaea lotus*), rising above water filled with fish and waterfowl. (This is not to be confused with the tall Indian lotus depicted on page 143.)

Around the pool, considerably out of scale with the waterlilies, are a few rushes and some papyrus plants (symbol of rebirth), which one imagines would have been grown in a separate bed filled with wet mud around the pool itself – the tall papyrus must have rather impeded an overall view of the water. The conical trees are the sycamore fig (*Ficus sycomorus*), a warm-country relation of the common fig, depicted alternately in fruit and showing a pattern of dark branches. Most of the palm trees in between are date palms (*Phoenix dactylifera*), staple utilitarian tree of Egypt, but the palm at top right seems to be the forking doum palm (*Hyphaene thebaica*). The spreading shrub at bottom left is probably a grape vine.

The bushy plant prominent at top left is a bit of a mystery. Although it looks like some kind of low-growing palm, there is no palm of that habit in Egypt, and it has been suggested that it is a mandrake (*Mandragora officinarum*), drawn very much out of scale, like the papyrus. This Mediterranean plant, with many associations in mythology and folklore and used in ancient times as a narcotic, does have orange fruits, sweetish and not unpleasant to eat.

It would be easy to reproduce an Egyptian garden like this in a small rectangular plot, and what is more, the idea of a wet border around the pool itself has possibilities. This is something seemingly never carried out in water gardens today, but what a good idea to allow cultivation of bog plants and 'marginals', such as marsh marigold (*Caltha*), flowering rush (*Butomus*), bogbean (*Menyanthes*) and *Lobelia cardinalis*.

The trees in the Egyptian painting are treated in a rigidly stylized manner, planted at exact intervals, but in a real garden they would probably be a few feet from the outer wall, providing room for growth and access to the poolside. A number of conifers, notably varieties of Lawson's cypress (*Chamaecyparis lawsoniana*), have the same outline as sycamore figs, or one could choose from the numerous fastigiate or upright forms of orthodox trees, including beech, crab apple, ornamental cherry, tulip tree, mountain ash and maple.

THE EMPEROR BABUR LAYING OUT A GARDEN AT KABUL

Bishandas, c. 1600

LONDON (VICTORIA AND ALBERT MUSEUM)

The first Mughul Emperor, Babur, made his 'Garden of Fidelity', probably at Nimla near Kabul, Afghanistan, in 1508–9. It is a traditional *chahar bagh* or garden in four parts. This plan is based on the 'cosmic cross', a symbol of several religions, which makes its first appearance in print in Genesis: 'And a river went out of Eden to water the garden; and from thence it was parted, and became into four heads.' In ancient Persia this device is reflected in their famous carpets, which have rivers in a cross pattern and four or eight garden divisions in each quadrant. The Mughuls adopted the Koranic Garden of Paradise of the Moslems with its eight divisions, but usually kept their gardens to the simpler four parts.

Babur's own words describe the making of this garden. 'I laid out the Four-gardens, known as the Bagh-i Wafa, on a rising ground, facing south . . . There oranges, citrons and pomegranates grow in abundance . . . I had plantains [bananas] brought and planted there; they did very well. The year before, I had sugar-cane planted there; it also did well . . . The garden lies high, has running water close at hand, and a mild winter climate. In the middle of it, a one-mill stream flows constantly past the little hill on which there are the four garden-plots. In the south-west part of it there is a reservoir 10 by 10 yards, round which are orange trees and a few pomegranates, the whole encircled by a trefoil meadow. This is the best part of the garden, a most beautiful sight when the oranges take colour. Truly that garden is admirably situated.'

In the picture here Babur, kept cool by a retainer behind, seems to be discussing a point with his engineer, or designer, who is holding a plan. Two men hold a line to ensure a straight edge, and another holds the surplus. Two more artisans are holding interestingly shaped spades. At the lower left of the picture, visitors seem to be acclaiming the Emperor and his work.

There are various plants in the beds, probably annual flowers, and around the four-parted design are the pomegranates and citrus trees already mentioned.

I do not know of any replica of a Mughul garden of this kind, but it would certainly be an interesting 'conceit'. The solid-walled beds could be almost as small or large as the space allowed, filled with annuals, dwarf shrubs or perhaps herbs. The water cross could be static and contain plants – water irises and arum lilies would be appropriate – or a pump at the central point could circulate water to and from a lower tank, as in Babur's original design.

A narrow, raised canal, with a waterfall,
gives an exotic feel to a town garden.

THE GARDEN OF THE FAIRIES

India – Mughul period, c. 1595

LONDON (VICTORIA AND ALBERT MUSEUM)

This delightful miniature illustrates the poetical romance, *Mrigavat,* written in 1501. The lady in the water, remonstrating with a prince, had previously appeared before him, in the guise of a doe which he was hunting. He waited by the lake into which the doe had plunged, where at his request his father built a temple. When the princess returned for a religious festival he stole her magic clothes so that she could not escape as her companions are doing; but all ended well, for on his declaration of his love for her she agreed to marry him.

The painting also depicts various aspects of the Mughul garden of the time of the Emperor Akbar, in the second half of the 16th century. The Mughuls, invading from Afghanistan, had a predominantly Persian gardening tradition. Some of their large gardens were four-parted, like Babur's famous Bagh-i-Wafa (shown on page 139); others had huge oblong canals, like the hillside masterpieces of Kashmir, or had pavilions built in the middle of a lake.

The smaller gardens would be like this one, entirely secluded and featuring flower-filled beds around a large rectangular 'tank', as such pools were called in India, in which the ladies of the household could disport themselves. Bathing tanks were normally clear (see page 143); the one here seems to have been designed for tropical waterlilies and wildfowl rather than for swimming.

The pavilion here is built to one side of the water, and forms part of the enclosing building where an open landing, beautifully carpeted, faces on to the pool garden, the doors behind opening into the rooms of the household.

The shrub in the centre of the picture may be the Shrub Althaea, *Hibiscus syriacus,* native to eastern Asia; the blotched flowers certainly resemble some present-day garden varieties. However, the same flowers can be seen on the leafy herbaceous plant at the right of the picture, so perhaps most of the plants depicted are heavily stylized. The leafy trees on either side of the shrub are undoubtedly plantains – bananas of some kind.

The enclosed garden is very much an eastern conception, reflecting a lifestyle where the women seldom leave the house, but it also produces an oasis of greenery, shutting off the hot, dusty world outside. In these enclosed gardens water is a vital ingredient. Often moving with fountains, but here a placid reservoir, it created an inviting coolness.

Such combinations of water, coolness, shade and greenery in enclosed gardens were found in most hot eastern civilizations, and was brought to Spain by the Moors, as the painting of the Garden of the Generalife shows on page 85.

Pools are used increasingly in gardens today, especially the swimming pool in congenial climates. In a large garden the swimming pool is ideally enclosed within sheltering walls or hedges, with a pavilion for changing and recreation alongside, and a terrace on which plant containers can stand. The plants can be formal, like bay trees or erect conifers or exotic, like agaves or daturas, or floriferous, like fuchsias and a host of other attractive, bright-flowered bedding plants.

Grouped large-leaved plants

INDIAN PRINCESS IN A GARDEN

18th century Rajput miniature (detail)

India has a long history of fine gardens (starting around the 4th century BC) in which there were formal pools (known as 'tanks') surrounded by buildings, beds of plants, and groves of trees. The Buddhists made gardens as places of retreat and in the 15th century, when the Mughuls invaded India, their first Emperor, Babur, made many such gardens, like his Garden of Fidelity (illustrated on page 139).

The style of gardening established by the Mughuls was developed, after the end of their dynasty, by the rulers of Rajputana (north-west India) and the Deccan (Bombay), who incorporated many features from earlier Hindu tradition into their gardens. We see here a Rajput garden, where a reclining princess receives refreshment from a retainer, while, on the right, a visitor greets her. This is the *zenana* or women's abode, its main terraces spread with beautifully worked carpets.

The garden is made in a flat plain; beyond the water there is probably an artificial lake, or possibly a river. In various ways the garden plan is like that of the splendid Mughul gardens of Kashmir, but without the advantage of their natural slope, which allows water to pass from the mountain streams above down through rectangular canals and over cascades. But there is moving water here in the form of the fountains – three in a row in a small pool beside the further pavilion and one in the centre of the bigger pool, which is probably the ladies' bathing 'tank'. Behind the three smaller fountains the blue rectangle in the wall under the pavilion is probably a vertical cascade, making that further part of the garden musical with the sound of falling water and pleasantly cool from the spray.

In the foreground another fountain cascades into a pool filled with lotus lilies, a favourite water plant of India and a Buddhist symbol as well, with its huge circular leaves and great cup-shaped, multi-petalled flowers held above the water on long stems.

The beds beyond are filled with flowers, set off by small palms and cypresses. They would include cannas, balsams, marigolds, amaranth, coleus and perhaps hollyhocks. In due course, as introductions from the New World reached the East, there would be zinnias, cosmeas, Achimenes and exotic-leaved caladiums as well.

Beyond the reddish walls are close-packed groves of trees; cypresses and bananas are discernible among the native Indian trees favoured by gardeners of that time, grown for both foliage and flower, and for sweet-scented blooms whenever possible.

We are probably looking at this garden in July, the time of summer rains and the one month of the year, when the ladies of the palace went into their gardens by day, and when the flowers in the beds were at their best. Otherwise, Hindu ladies apparently went out at night only, preferring to see their gardens by moonlight when presumably the temperature was more bearable.

MAISON DE PLAISANCE

Anon, 19th century

LONDON (BRITISH LIBRARY)

Gardening has been going on in China for well over 2,000 years. Its origins lie partly in the tracts of country set aside by rulers for hunting, which gradually became complexes with palaces, temples, specially planted trees, and areas where animals were kept, and partly in the monasteries with their numerous courtyards, which developed at the same time. The latter were perhaps the strongest influence on smaller private estates of the kind seen in this French engraving, showing a garden of a type which continued from around the 4th century right into the 19th.

Buildings, courtyards and gardens are all linked by a landscape of rocks, a lake, and distant mountains beyond. Some of the early Chinese landscape gardens relied almost entirely on the natural landscape, and here the surreal-looking groups of stones might be natural – such bizarre outcrops do occur in China – but could equally well have been erected. The latter seems more likely in view of the portico with the red door, which probably leads to an artificial cavern. This was a recorded feature from some ancient gardens, and a further obviously man-made feature is the flight of steps among the rocks, which emerges on a precarious-looking rock platform complete with a pavilion in which to sit and admire the view.

A bridge – zigzagged to prevent evil spirits crossing – leads to the further shore of the lake, where other buildings are placed for various kinds of recreation. One oddity in this landscape is the curious tower on the horizon at mid-left, which looks like the top of a pagoda or Buddhist temple, and recalls some English landscape gardens which have obelisks or towers placed in a way that enhances a distant view.

Each courtyard is a garden in its own right, and nearly all contain the groups of stones that are a characteristic of Chinese gardens, and can still be seen today, notably in Suzhou. They are waterworn rocks from Lake Wusih, and they became a passion with the Chinese garden-makers. Stones represented mountains and were the repository of magic powers, reminding us of the complex symbolism behind all Chinese gardens.

On a more down-to-earth level, we can see that the courtyards vary in size, presenting the visitor with a series of individual, unexpected tableaux. Plants are few. The trees in bloom are mostly magnolias, and there is a flowering cherry to the left. In the centre courtyard a low plant with large flowers is almost certainly a peony, prized by the Chinese since early times.

Gardeners satisfied with a somewhat ascetic layout could recreate an 'outdoor room' in Chinese style with paving, gravel or cobbles, some big boulders, an attractively shaped tree and a clump of bamboo.

Simple plank bridge over a stream.

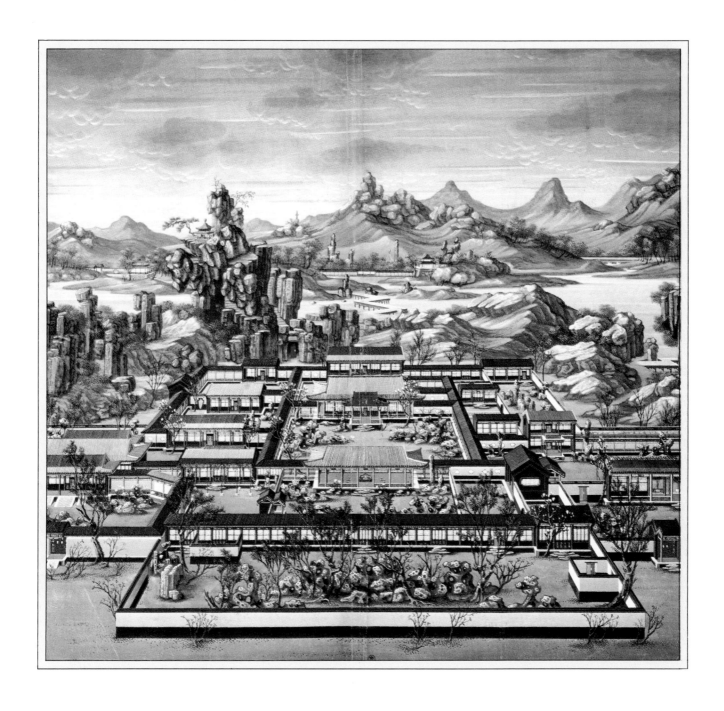

LANDSCAPE GARDEN

Chinese, 19th century

WASHINGTON (FREER GALLERY)

This garden detail, part of a scroll illustrating a romantic story, will be recognizable to anyone who has seen the gardens of Suzhou (Soochow) or indeed studied books of existing Chinese gardens. In these the typical layout is based on water, around which is a sequence of buildings, paths, bridges and open galleries, so that a visitor can walk around looking at the ways in which different features are reflected in the water. In between, they could pause in the buildings designated for various special purposes – to observe fish, to read, to compose poetry or take tea perhaps.

The pavilion projecting over the water here, in which a lady carries out her toilette, is comparable to the basic structure in a Chinese garden, the *t'ing,* a free-standing open-sided pavilion. There is indeed a Chinese saying that once a place has a *t'ing,* it can be called a garden. Most garden pavilions are rather more ornate than this one, and the bridges and balustrades all have different patterns.

Water is an essential element in any Chinese garden; it represents the feminine *yang* whereas the *yin,* its male complement, is embodied in the waterworn limestone rocks prized by Chinese gardeners (one such rock appears at the right of our picture). As spelt out in detail on page 144, these rocks also represent mountains and are the repository of *mana,* or magic force. 'Digging ponds and making mountains' was a common Chinese phrase for making a garden, in which nature is interpreted rather than represented. There is a nice saying, too, from Confucius: 'The wise man delights in water, the good man delights in mountains. For the wise move but the good stay still. The wise are happy but the good secure.'

In this garden, too, is part of a gnarled old pine, whose rugged growth symbolized natural wildness; it might be contrasted, as elsewhere in this scroll, with the fresh upspringing leaves of a banana, as age compared with youth (though the banana is also a symbol of scholarly ambition); or with delicately leaved bamboo, maple with its autumn colour, or flowering cherries or peaches.

The water is filled with Indian lotus, prized as much by the Chinese as by the Indians (page 142), which transforms the surface of the garden lakes from reflecting mirrors in springtime, often completely hiding the surface in summer. The plant-entwined trellis here is another favoured seasonal device, for as the year wears on the flowers cover it. Here they are probably small cluster-flowered roses.

In China, painting and gardening were parallel pursuits. There is a quotation that a garden is 'a scroll painting you enter in fancy', doubly apt in the case of this detail of a scroll. A Chinese garden is composed of a multitude of small compartments and features, always with the suggestion of something enticing further on; and, like a scroll which is unfurled a section at a time, each small piece of garden is meant to be savoured individually. A relatively simple idea to copy in a modified form and one which could transform a garden that otherwise lacked interesting contours or specially attractive features.

HAND-SCROLL

Tang Yifen, 19th century

LONDON (BRITISH LIBRARY)

*E*verything about this Chinese garden is informal, with irregular, flowing lines – a great contrast to that shown on page 145. We can, in fact, see perhaps half the garden, because the outer wall goes out of the picture at bottom left and at mid-right. On the upper right is a dwelling complex, with perhaps farm buildings beyond it, for this appears to be very much a country garden.

The outer wall, an open gallery with pavilions strung along it, made it possible to walk right round the garden under shelter, pausing in the pavilions to view the natural scenery beyond – a river on the left or the various features of the garden within.

A fairly rustic garden, it might have been made by a scholar rather than an aristocrat or administrator. Most of the left-hand part of the view is the all-important lake. At the bottom on the left a little wooden bridge crosses an inlet, and from the path one could climb the rocky central knoll with its simple pavilion at the viewpoint.

The main path continues via another bridge over an inlet – this one with a pergola clothed in a creeper – to a rather more complex area. It has an isolated pavilion for recreation, a small sitting pavilion in an enclosure with a serpentine wicker fence on one side and on the other a wall pierced by a moongate, an item of Chinese garden-craft popular in the West. Three discreet groups of waterworn rocks can be seen near the larger pavilion, and there is a rectangular fenced garden close to the buildings with a formal flower bed in it. To the right of this bed, a raised plank holds two examples of *penjing*, miniature landscapes which the Japanese developed into the better-known *bonsai*. One is a contorted dwarf tree in a large ceramic pot, the other a stone landscape of pinnacle rocks.

Such dwarf trees retain their miniature habit by root constriction and trimming accompanied by detailed mini-pruning and shaping of the top growth. They are best displayed on a raised stone bench or slatted wooden staging. In winter they may need the protection of a cool greenhouse (with minimal heating) to prevent severe frost killing the roots in their shallow containers.

This garden contains several larger examples of *penjing* trees, for they did not have to be tiny, as well as some more natural trees and a big grove of bamboos in the foreground.

A SCREEN

Anon (Japan)

(PRIVATE COLLECTION)

The Japanese garden owes it origins to the Chinese, and to the influence of the highly artistic T'ang period (AD 618-907). But initial Chinese inspiration has been refined to the point where the placement of a rock, or of flat pebbles under water, or of the alignment of stepping stones, is enormously important. Although the traditional elements can be adapted, the influence of Buddhism, and a reverence for natural things often stated symbolically, are a constant, underlying factor.

The Japanese garden, like those of the temples, appears to be frozen in time. Once such gardens reached maturity, the shrubs in them were clipped to retain their outlines, and the trees pruned twig by twig so that they retained a constant shape.

This screen painting shows some of the basic ingredients of Japanese gardens – the flowering cherries, a clipped pine with pillow-like tiers of foliage and a grassy or mossed mound in the foreground. The rest of the garden to be viewed from the characteristic wooden pavilion is left to the imagination.

The traditional Japanese garden usually includes certain 'hard' ingredients – stone lanterns, carefully placed rocks, mounded moss, raked gravel, clipped shrubs and trees, irregular pools and meandering streams, islands, arched bridges, stepping stones across water or a 'dry stream' of cobblestones, discreet waterfalls and fountains, and paved walks. The austere gardens of Zen Buddhist temples can consist entirely of raked sand or gravel with rocks like islands, but most Japanese gardens are very individualistic, combining both the conventional 'props' and others in an infinite number of ways.

Flowers like those of an English border are subsidiary items, carefully positioned to provide grace-notes in each season. Most of the colour comes from a succession of flowering trees, shrubs and a few long-lived perennials – camellias, cherries, apricots, azaleas, wisteria, peonies, irises, lilies, chrysanthemums – and Indian lotus in the pools. Maples and cherries provide glorious autumn foliage colours before the conifers hold sway in the leafless winter.

Creating a Japanese garden calls for careful study of the originals and a similarly subtle approach. For those who can do without the brilliance of constantly changing flowering plants, and the shabby growth that often follows, such a garden can be intensely satisfying, and the small town or suburban plot is well suited to it. To disguise the typical fence or wall of western plots, split bamboo screens can be very effective. A wooden deck between the house and the garden is a useful way of separating Western architecture from the oriental design of the garden and a Japanese-style pavilion can be erected at the other end of the plot.

Typical Japanese statuary.

BIOGRAPHIES OF PAINTERS

E. ADVENO BROOKE FL. 1844-64

A painter of landscapes, fishing and river subjects, Brooke lived in London and exhibited at the Royal Academy and elsewhere.

ERNEST ALBERT CHADWICK 1876-

A watercolourist, Chadwick concentrated on landscapes, exhibiting at the Royal Academy and all the principal galleries during his lifetime.

MARTIN CHARLOT B. 1944

Known primarily as an oil painter and a muralist working in the fresco technique, Charlot's compositions are figurative. He often depicts the people of Hawaii, where he now works. A careful draughtsman, his paintings are a combination of accurate detail and surrealism. He has exhibited in the De Mena Gallery, New York City and in the Contemporary Arts Center, Honolulu.

JEAN COTELLE (LE JEUNE) 1642-1708

Born in Paris in 1642, Cotelle was received into the Academy for his miniature of 'L'Entree du roi at de la reine dans Paris', and finally became a lecturer at the Academy in 1704. His works hang in Versailles and in Leningrad.

EDMOND BYRNE DE SATUR FL. 1878-1885

A London painter, de Satur concentrated on domestic subjects, exhibiting at the Royal Academy (from 1878-85) and elsewhere.

GEORGE SAMUEL ELGOOD 1851-1943

A watercolourist of landscape and architectural subjects, Elgood specialized in painting English and American gardens, but also spent several months of each year studying and painting in Italy.

CHARLES GIRAUD 1819-1892

Born in Paris in 1819, Giraud was trained by his elder brother and was also a pupil at the Ecole des Beaux Arts in Paris. He travelled widely during his career, and was commissioned as a war painter by the Government of the time, and was also the official painter of a scientific expedition to Iceland and Greenland in the mid-19th century. The paintings now hang in the Natural History Museum in Paris. In later years he became a distinguished 'salon' painter, and specialized in depicting sumptuous Parisian interiors. One of his paintings hangs in the Louvre.

ANTHONY GREEN B. 1939

A former student of the Slade School of Fine Art in London (from 1956-60), Green concentrates on oils and pencil drawings. He has had exhibitions at the Bristol Museum and Art Gallery, at the Arnolfini Gallery in Bristol and in Berlin, and he has also exhibited at the Royal Academy.

ABEL GRIMMER FL. C. 1595

Born in Anvers in 1573, Abel Grimmer was the son of the painter, Jakob. His works are similar to, and often confused with, those of Sebastien Vrancz (q.v.). He was received into the guild of painters in 1592. His paintings are now hanging in museums in Anvers, Brussels and Rotterdam.

WINSLOW HOMER 1836-1910

Born in Boston, in the USA, Homer was primarily a marine and genre painter, but also painted rural and domestic scenes. He was apprenticed to a lithographer before studying in New York and Paris, becoming artist to *Harper's Weekly* during the Civil War. He was best known for his seascapes, some of which are exhibited in the Metropolitan Museum of Art, in New York.

GUSTAV KLIMT 1862-1918

Born in Vienna, Klimt eventually became a major member of the Art Nouveau movement, whose work influenced Munch, Toulouse-Lautrec and Gauguin. Klimt spent much of his time designing for the theatre, but he also exhibited in Paris in 1900. A number of his works hang in the museum in Munich.

JOHN FREDERICK LEWIS 1805-1876

A painter and watercolourist of landscapes and animals, Lewis came from a family of painters – both his father and his uncle were artists. He studied animals under Landseer and began to exhibit his own work in 1820, turning to watercolours in 1825. In 1850 his watercolour *The Harem* created a sensation and he was hailed by Ruskin as a leading pre-Raphaelite. He returned to oil painting again in 1858. An exhibition of his work was held at the Royal Academy in 1934.

EDOUARD MANET 1832-83

Earmarked for a legal career, Manet took up painting instead. His work was considered too provocative by the classicists of his period, and he exhibited at the Salon de Refusés instead, along with Monet, Renoir and other rebels, helping to form the group out of which the Impressionist movement arose. His later canvases are more markedly impressionistic.

CLAUDE MONET 1840-1926

Monet was born in Paris but spent his youth in Le Havre, where he met Boudin, who encouraged him to paint out of doors. He later moved to Paris, where he became friendly with Renoir, Pissarro and Sisley, and exhibited at the first Impressionist Exhibition with them in 1874. He visited England, Holland and Venice, spending his life finding different ways of expressing the nuances of colour, atmosphere and light in the landscape. The latter part of his life was spent at his house at Giverny, where a number of studies of the *Bassin aux Nymphaeas* were painted.

SAMUEL PALMER 1805-81

Primarily a landscape painter and etcher, Samuel Palmer was born in London. He was much influenced by his friend William Blake and is best known for his watercolours. Not popular during his lifetime, Palmer's work now achieves the acclaim it deserves.

ERIC RAVILIOUS 1908-42

A student of the Royal College of Art, where he later became a lecturer, Ravilious illustrated a number of books, as well as producing designs for pottery and glassware. He is also well known for his scenes from the 1939-45 War, and a number of his works now hang in the Tate Gallery in London.

HUMPHRY REPTON 1752-1818

A writer, landscape architect and painter, Repton exhibited at the Royal Academy from 1787 to 1802. He started as a landscape designer in 1788, deliberately setting out to be the successor to 'Capability' Brown, though he soon developed a very personal style and approach. He designed the parks at Cobham, Woburn and Richmond, and modified Kensington Gardens. The Victoria and Albert Museum has a number of his watercolours.

W. T. RICHARDS 1833-1905

Born in Philadelphia, Richards travelled to Europe in 1855 and visited Florence, Rome and Paris. One of the foremost American painters to adopt the Pre-Raphaelite style, Richards became an honorary member of the National Academy of New York, as well as exhibiting in Paris and in London, at the Royal Academy.

THOMAS ROBINS (THE ELDER) D. C. 1770

Often confused with his namesake son, who painted flower pieces, Robins the Elder was much in demand as a painter of gardens by landowners who wished to make a record of the improvements they had made to their properties. Largely neglected after his death, his work is now increasingly valued for its record of the gardening details of the time.

HENRI ROUSSEAU 1844-1910

Most of Rousseau's life was spent as a minor customs official earning him the nickname 'Le Douanier'. He retired in 1885 and spent his time painting and copying at the Louvre. From 1886 to 1898, and from 1901 to 1910, he exhibited at the Salon des Indépendants. He is best known for exotic imaginary landscapes with trees and plants.

ERNEST ARTHUR ROWE 1863-1922

A landscape painter, Rowe lived in Lambeth and in Tunbridge Wells, exhibiting at the Royal Academy and elsewhere from 1885 onwards. The Greatorex Galleries in Grafton Street, London, held a one man show of his watercolours in 1921.

PETER PAUL RUBENS 1577-1640

A diplomat as well as a painter, Rubens travelled in both Spain and Italy painting both court and religious scenes. After the death of his first wife, he married Helena Fourment in 1630 and retired to his estate at Steen, where he concentrated on landscape painting. He produced more than 1200 works in his lifetime, many of the best ones hanging in Antwerp, where he was educated and then lived, between diplomatic missions.

DAVID RYDER FL. 1848

Very little seems to be known about David Ryder, to whom the painting of Arabella Sparrow has been attributed. It has been suggested that the skilled handling of the foliage, compared with the rather stiff treatment of the little girl in this painting indicates that he was more accustomed to wall murals or ornamental painting, rather than portraiture. The painting has been exhibited at the Abby Aldrich Rockefeller Folk Art Center, Colonial Williamsburg Foundation in the 1970s, and published in the *Middleborough Antiquarian*, Vol XVIII in April 1978.

PIETER ANDREAS RYSBRACK 1684-1748

A painter of still life, landscapes and animals, Rysbrack was born in Paris into a family of artists. His father was a well-known Antwerp landscape painter and his two brothers were also artists.

PAUL SANDBY 1730-1809

Born in Nottingham in 1730, Sandby specialized in landscape, mainly in watercolour and gouache. The brother of the architect, Thomas Sandby, he became one of the pioneers of the natural English landscape painting and a popular teacher of drawing. The largest collection of his works is at Windsor Castle.

EMIL JACOB SCHINDLER 1842-92

Born in Vienna, Schindler became a student under Zimmerman at the Vienna Academy. His interest in nature led him towards the French school and he was much influenced by Rousseau and Corot. A member of the Academy of Vienna, he held a number of decorations. His works are on show in Museums in Berlin, Leipzig and Munich, as well as in Vienna.

STANLEY SPENCER 1891-1959

Born at Cookham, Spencer studied at the Slade School of Fine Art. From 1926 to 1933 he executed murals in the Oratory of All Souls at Burghclere. Although his main works are of religious subjects, he also produced a number of landscapes. He was elected to the Royal Academy in 1950 and knighted nine years later.

KARL SPITZWEG 1808-85

Spitzweg began his career as a chemist, but took up painting instead, in such earnest that he was exhibiting by 1836. He travelled in France and England, and his works are highly regarded in Germany for their painterly qualities and wonderful attention to detail.

DAVID SUFF B. 1955

A student of Leeds University and the Royal College of Art, Suff has also taught etching and travelled extensively. His work is a regular feature of the Royal Academy Summer Exhibition and he has also had one-man exhibitions at the Piccadilly Gallery in 1983 and 1986, and figured in the Hayward Annual Exhibition in 1982.

LOUIS TURPIN B. 1947

Trained at Falmouth School of Art, Turpin has had several one-man shows, including a recent one at the Beaux Arts Gallery in Bath. A keen painter of gardens, he was first attracted to the subject by Sissinghurst Castle, Vita Sackville-West's garden in Kent.

VINCENT VAN GOGH 1835-90

The son of a pastor, van Gogh worked on leaving school for a firm of art dealers in The Hague, London and Paris. After several attempts at different careers, and a couple of failed love affairs, he began to study art in Paris, where he met Gauguin, Toulouse-Lautrec and Seurat. He left Paris in 1888 to paint the Provencale landscape, where he produced many of his best loved works. After his much publicised quarrel with Gauguin, he became an inmate at the Asylum at St Rémy. In 1890 he went to Auvers-sur-Oise under the supervision of Dr. Paul Gachet but, sadly, committed suicide in the summer of that year. One of the pioneers of Expressionism, Van Gogh had a profound influence on the Fauves.

SEBASTIEN VRANCZ 1573-1647

Born in Anvers, where he died at the age of 74, Vrancz was a member of the Flemish school, who depicted with great verve the daily life of the time. He travelled to Italy but remained true to the Flemish painting tradition. His works hang in museums and galleries in Amsterdam, Anvers, Paris and Vienna, amongst others.

EDOUARD VUILLARD 1868-1940

Strongly influenced by Gauguin and the vogue for Japanese painting, Vuillard was also influenced by Bonnard, with whom he shared a studio in Paris. He is best known for his interiors and his flower pieces, with their wonderful feeling for light and colour. He died at La Baule in 1940.

SUE WALL B. 1950

Born in Ohio, and a student at the university there, Sue Wall has won numerous awards, as well as exhibiting in one-woman shows in Ohio, New York, Florida and Kansas. Her work can be seen in several museums and galleries in the USA.

JOHANN JAKOB WALTHER FL. 1625-75

Born in Saxony around 1600, Walther died in Strasbourg some time after 1679. His works are to be found in the Bibliothèque Provinciale de Darmstadt and the Bibliothèque Nationale de Paris.

SELECTED PLANT LIST

(Compiled by Nigel Colborn)
Examples of some of the plants that were in cultivation from Roman times until the twentieth century. Although this list is far from complete, it shows a *selection* of what gardeners were growing through the ages until recent times. For long stretches of horticultural history, flowering plants were grown not for the beauty of their flowers but for more mundane needs, such as cooking or medicine.

(spp. = several species)

ROMAN TIMES
Acanthus spinosus
Arbutus unedo Strawberry Tree
Buxus sempervirens Box
Centaurea cyanus Cornflower
Cheiranthus spp. Wallflower
Chrysanthemum spp.
Citrus spp.
Corylus maxima Filbert
Cupressus sempervirens Cypress
Genista tinctoria Dyers' Greenweed
Hedera helix Ivy
Humulus lupulus Hop
Iris florentina Orris
Laurus nobilis Bay
Lilium candidum Madonna Lily
Lonicera periclymenum Honeysuckle
Myrtus communis Myrtle
Nerium oleander Oleander
Papaver spp. Poppies
Phyllitis scolopendrium Fern
Platanus orientalis Oriental Plane
Punica granatum Pomegranate
Rosa spp.
Rosmarinus officinalis Rosemary
Ruscus aculeatus Butchers' Broom
Salvia spp. Sages
Thymus vulgaris Thyme
Viburnum tinus
Viola odorata Sweet Violet

ROMAN FRUIT
Apples
Cherries
Dates
Figs
Grapes
Lemons
Olives
Pears
Plums
Pomegranates
Strawberries
Hazel Nuts

FROM ROME TO 1500 AD
Many of the Roman plants must have stayed in cultivation though some were lost until re-introduced later. Examples of plants in Europe that survived the Dark Ages are as follows:

Artemisia abrotanum Lad's Love
Borago officinalis Borage
Crocus sativus Saffron
Dianthus spp. Pinks and Carnations
Fritillaria imperialis Crown Imperial
Helleborus niger Christmas Rose
Hepatica triloba
Iris florentina Orris
Iris germanica
Laurus nobilis Bay
Lavandula spica Lavender
Lavandula stoechas French Lavender
Lilium candidum Madonna Lily
Rosa spp. Roses
Santolina chamaecyparissus Cotton Lavender
Teucrium chamaedrys Germander
Thymus vulgaris Thyme

SIXTEENTH CENTURY EUROPE
European origin unless marked:
A - Africa. As - Asia. Aus - Australia.
NA - North America. SA - South America

Acanthus mollis Bear's Breeches
Aconitum napellus Monkshood
Aesculus hippocastanum Horse Chestnut
Allium moly
Althaea rosea Hollyhock (As)
Anemone coronaria Poppy aenemone
Asphodeline lutea
Aster amellus (NA)
Calamintha grandiflora
Campanula persicifolia
Cercis siliquastrum Judas Tree (As)
Cornus mas Cornelian Cherry
Crocus aureus
Cyclamen coum
Dianthus plumarius
Dianthus spp.
Dianthus superbus

Dictamnus albus Dittany
Doronicum caucasicum Leopardsbane
Eranthis hyemalis Winter Aconite
Geranium macrorrhizum
Hemerocallis spp. Day Lily (As)
Hesperis matronalis Sweet Rocket
Hyacinthus orientalis Hyacinth (As)
Iris pallida (As)
Laburnum alpinum
Lavatera olbia Tree Mallow
Lilium martagon Turks Cap Lily
Lunaria biennis Honesty
Narcissus jonquilla Jonquil
Phillyrea angustifolia (A)
Phlomis fruticosa Jerusalem Sage
Quercus ilex Holm Oak
Scorzonera spp.
Thuja occidentalis Arbor vitae (NA)

SEVENTEENTH CENTURY EUROPE
Acer negundo Box Elder (NA)
Acer rubrum (NA)
Achillea taygetea (As)
Actaea spicata Baneberry (NA)
Agapanthus spp. Nile Lily (A)
Alyssum olympicum
Anchusa angustifolia
Antirrhinum spp. Snapdragon
Aquilegia canadensis Canadian Columbine (NA)
Aster tradescantii (NA)
Cedrus libani Cedar of Lebanon
Chrysanthemum frutescens Marguerite (Canary isl)
Erica arborea Tree Heather (A)
Erythronium americanum Trout Lily (NA)
Gladiolus byzantinus (A)
Lathyrus vernus Spring Vetchling
Liriodendron tulipifera Tulip Tree (NA)
Lobelia cardinalis Cardinal Flower (NA)
Mertensia spp. (NA)
Nerine sarniensis Guernsey Lily (A)
Prunus lusitanica
Prunus tenella
Rhododendron hirsutum (First in cultivation 1656)
Sassafras albidum (NA)
Syringa x persica Lilac (As)
Tropaeolum majus Nasturtium (SA)
Tulipa clusiana Lady Tulip (As)
Zephyranthes spp. Flower of the Western Wind (NA)

EIGHTEENTH CENTURY EUROPE

Alstroemeria spp. (SA)
Aquilegia alpina
Araucaria araucana Monkey Puzzle (SA)
Asparagus officinalis Asparagus
Aster novi-angliae (NA)
Aster novi-belgii Michaelmas Daisy (NA)
Aubrieta deltoides (As)
Aucuba japonica Spotted Laurel (As)
Baptisia australis (NA)
Berberis spp. (SA)
Bergenia spp. (As)
Buddleia globosa (SA)
Callistemon spp. Bottlebrush (Aus)
Camellia japonica (As)
Ceanothus spp. (NA)
Centaurea acaulis (As)
Chrysanthemum alpinum
Chrysanthemum balsamita Alecost (As)
Chrysanthemum indicum hybds (As)
Cimicifuga foetida (As)
Dahlia spp. (SA)
Franklinia alatamaha (NA)
Gaillardia spp. (NA)
Geum virginianum (NA)
Hydrangea arborescens (NA)
Kalmia latifolia Mountain Laurel (NA)
Kniphofia spp. Red Hot Pokers (A)
Leptospermum lanigerum Tea Tree (Aus)
Lupinus spp. Lupins (NA)
Lysimachia spp.
Magnolia grandiflora (NA)
Paeonia suffruticosa Tree Peony (As)
Papaver orientale Oriental Poppy (As)
Penstemon spp. (NA)
Phlox spp. (NA)
Phormium tenax New Zealand Flax (New Zealand)
Rhododendron maximum (NA)
Rubus odoratus Flowering Bramble (NA)
Solidago spp. Goldenrods (NA)
Trillium grandiflorum Wakerobin (NA)

NINETEENTH CENTURY AMERICA

The following lists a few examples of plants grown in North American gardens between the War for Independence and the end of the nineteenth century.

Acer negundo Box Elder
Aconitum spp. Monkshood
Actaea spp. Bane Berry
Adiantum pedatum Maidenhair Fern

Agave Century Plant
Ailanthus altissima Tree of Heaven
Alstroemeria spp.
Anemone spp.
Althaea rosea Hollyhock
Amaranthus spp.
Aquilegia spp. Columbines
Anthemis nobilis Chamomile
Arbutus unedo Strawberry Tree
Arisaema dracontium
Aristolochia macrophylla Dutchman's Pipe
Aster virginiana
Betula spp. Birches
Canna indica Indian Shot
Capparis spinosa Caper
Catalpa bignonioides Indian Bean
Coreopsis verticillata
Cotton
Custard Apple
Cytisus spp. Broom
Dodecatheon media Shooting Star
Linum spp. Flax
Fothergilla alnifolia Witch Alder
Gaillardia spp.
Galega officinalis Goat's Rue
Gardenia spp.
Halesia carolina Snowdrop Tree
Helianthus multiflorus
Hibiscus spp.
Iberis spp.
Iris versicolor
Jasminum spp.
Kalmia latifolia Mountain Laurel
Koelreuteria paniculata Golden Rain
Laburnum spp.
Lantana aculeata
Larix spp. Larches
Lathyrus odoratus Sweet Pea
Lavatera spp.
Lilium spp.
Liquidambar styraciflua
Magnolia spp.
Narcissus spp.
Nicotiana spp. Tobacco Plant
Oenothera spp. Evening Primroses
Ornithogalum spp. Star of Bethlehem
Ostrya virginiana Hop Hornbeam
Paeonia suffruticosa Tree Peony
Philadelphus spp. Mock Orange
Rubus odoratus
Rudbeckia spp.
Sarracenia spp. Pitcher Plant
Statice sinuata
Taxodium distichum Swamp Cypress

Viburnum spp.
Wisteria spp.

PLANTS BROUGHT INTO CULTIVATION IN TEMPERATE REGIONS 1800 TO 1850

Abies spp. (NA)
Anemone hupehensis (As)
Banksia oblongifolia (Aus)
Boronia (Aus)
Casuarina spp. (Aus)
Clarkia elegans (NA)
Clematis spp. (As), (NA), (Aus)
Delphinium cardinale (NA)
Eucalyptus glauca (Aus)
Garrya elliptica (NA)
Grevilea spp. Silk Oak (Aus)
Limnanthes douglasii (NA)
Mahonia aquifolium Oregon Grape (NA)
Picea sitchensis Sitka Spruce (NA)
Pinus contorta (NA)
Platycodon grandiflorum (As)
Rhododendron spp.
Ribes sanguineum (NA)
Sophora tomentosa (Aus)
Tecoma obliqua (Aus)

PLANTS BROUGHT INTO CULTIVATION IN TEMPERATE REGIONS 1850 TO 1900

Acer davidii (As)
Acer griseum Paperbark Maple (As)
Berberis spp. (SA)
Ceratostigma willmottiana (As)
Codonopsis farreri (As)
Daphne retusa (As)
Exochorda macrantha (As)
Gentiana sino-ornata (As)
Hamamelis mollis Witch Hazel (As)
Ligularia clivorum
Lilium delavayi (As)
Liriodendron chinense (As)
Lonicera fragrantissima (As)
Meconopsis simplicifolia (As)
Pleione spp. (As)
Primula spp. (As)
Rosa moyesii (As)
Rosa sericea (As)
Skimmia japonica (As)
Viburnum henryi (As)
Viburnum tomentosum (As)
Weigela florida (As)

ACKNOWLEDGMENTS

I am indebted to the following for advice, information and plant identification while working on this book: Departments of Egyptian, and of Oriental, Antiquities, British Museum; The Oriental Institute, University of Oxford; the Keeper of the Indian Department, Victoria & Albert Museum; members of staff, Royal Horticultural Society; Anthony Green; John Harris; Dr John Harvey; Arthur Hellyer; Allan Paterson; Mrs Helen Robinson; David Suff; Suttons Seeds Ltd; Christopher Thacker; and Graham Thomas.

ANTHONY HUXLEY

PICTURE CREDITS